Phra Farang

An English Monk in Thailand

Phra Peter Pannapadipo

Post Books

Phra Farang: An English Monk in Thailand
is published by Post Books
The Post Publishing Public Company Limited
136 Na Ranong Road, off Sunthorn Kosa Road
Klong Toey, Bangkok 10110, Thailand
Tel. (662) 240-3700 ext. 1691-2, Fax. (662) 671-9698
e-mail: postbooks@bangkokpost.net
http://www.bangkokpost.net/postbooks

©Phra Peter Pannapadipo 1997

First published in Thailand in November 1997
Second printing 1998
Printed in Thailand by Allied Printers
The Post Publishing Public Company Limited

National Library of Thailand Cataloging-in-Publication Data
Phra Peter Pannapadipo
   Phra Farang : An English Monk in Thailand.--2nd printing
   Bangkok : Post Books, 1997.
   242 p.
   1. Buddhist monks. I. Title. 294.30922

ISBN : 974-202-019-1

Editing: Helen Jandamit
Cover design: Watchara Ritmahan
Set in: Times, Tiffany, Brush Script

Author's preface

Nearly two years have elapsed between completing the manuscript of *Phra Farang: An English Monk in Thailand* and rereading for the final time prior to printing. In that time many of my ideas have changed or matured. I find, on re-reading the manuscript, that there are many points I would now prefer to express differently, or perhaps not to express at all. Some parts of the manuscript show a degree of naivety on my part, or at least a lack of understanding, and I have been tempted to revise them. On reflection, though, I have resisted making any major alterations at all. If parts of the book seem naive, it is because I was naive at the time of writing. But that naivety, or lack of understanding, is all part of my story—an essential part in fact.

When Buddhist monks write books it is their usual practice to dedicate any "merit" thereby accrued to others—often past teachers, living or dead. I'm not entirely convinced of the realities of "transferring merit", especially to dead people. Instead, I dedicate any author's royalties accrued towards the higher education of some of my impoverished Thai students, in the hope that they will have a brighter, better future in this lifetime.

Namo

Namo. Homage. Homage to the Buddha. The first word of a longer salutation at the beginning of every Buddhist service. But for me, personally, *Namo* means more than paying homage to the Buddha himself. It is also homage to the supreme effort he made to reach Enlightenment; to the sacrifices he made in rejecting his family and princely life-style; to the pain and suffering he endured as an ascetic before he discovered the 'Middle Way'. It is homage to the selfless devotion of 45 years of his life to teaching what he discovered—teaching all people regardless of creed or social status. It is homage to *what* he taught—the Dhamma; a shining beacon of wisdom that has drawn men and women for more than 2,500 years and lit the path to lead them from suffering. And it is homage to the Saṅgha; the community of monks and nuns that he created and who have devoted their lives to follow what he taught and who have preserved and practised the teaching for so many centuries, thus helping countless others along that difficult path.

Sometimes, when I am full of confidence, I picture the word with an exclamation mark. *Namo*! Proclaim it loudly throughout the world for the benefit of all mankind! But at other times; times of doubt in my strength and ability to follow, know, and live what the Buddha taught, there is a question mark. *Namo*? Then my mind is full of uncertainty which no amount of inward-seeking seems to answer.

I have chanted *Namo* with dozens of other monks in the most magnificent temples, kneeling on polished marble floors before gold-plated, jewel-encrusted images of staggering beauty, glittering in the light of huge candles and crystal chandeliers. Sometimes, then, it has just been a word—its own beauty seemingly diminished amongst the awesome but insignificant grandeur.

But also, late at night, sometimes feeling miserably lost and full of doubt, I have knelt alone on the dusty wooden floor of a simple little temple in Thailand's remote countryside before a cobweb-festooned image, gleaming dully in the light of a single candle. Then, my voice choked with emotion, I have whispered *Namo*, and bowed low before something so overwhelmingly vast and beautiful it is almost beyond comprehension. And my heart and mind have been uplifted and my strength has returned.

Namo Tassa Bhagavato Arahato Samma Sambuddhassa.
Homage to the Exalted One, Perfectly Enlightened by Himself.

Chapter 1

The first question most people ask me when we meet is "Why did you become a Buddhist monk?" I think they expect my answer to reveal some personal inadequacy, a dreadful tragedy in my past or some other dark secret. If that had been the case, I'd have joined the Foreign Legion. Becoming a Buddhist monk was — for me — not the result of running away from some personal darkness but rather progressing towards a great light.

I don't believe there was any one specific reason why I decided to ordain — I believe everything that ever happened to me, everything I ever did — good, bad or indifferent, from the moment of my birth, led in some small way to my eventual decision.

Looking back, a lot of my life seems to have been a waste of precious time. Although I certainly seemed to enjoy it then, with hindsight it wasn't even very interesting, not in any profound way. Like a lot of people, I was motivated by the baser senses and threw most of my time away on cheap thrills.

My parents were Christian so I suppose I was too in a vague way. I went to Sunday school as a child, to Christenings, weddings and funerals, and all the family attended 'special' services at the local church at Easter and Christmas. But somehow religion just sort of drifted out of my life. When I was about 16 'C of E' became something to write on official forms in the space for 'Religion'.

I was just about 40 years old when I started to re-evaluate my life. I had consciously made re-evaluations at other times too, of course, but they had been based on seeking change and improvement within the parameters of my existing lifestyle, rather than actually changing the whole way I viewed life and my role within it.

In all the previous years I had tried to live life to the full—or what I then thought of as 'full'. My lifestyle was neither extreme nor excessive, neither dishonest nor immoral, but I ducked and dived, wheeled and dealed my way through it, always seeking some new experience, some new thing to make it seem worthwhile. At the time I never questioned whether it was worthwhile or not. I was having fun and was far too busy to question its validity. As long as I had a heart full of dreams and a pocket full of money and could buy some transient happiness, that was all that seemed to matter. The idea of 'spiritual' satisfaction never really entered my head.

My life was not based solely on material acquisition or the pursuit of fleeting pleasures, for I actively, and at times successfully, sought strong emotional and long-term attachments. But even within my close personal relationships, I sometimes sensed that something was missing—there was an incompleteness'—and my relationships never seemed quite as fulfilling as other claimed *theirs* were. Perhaps there was some emotional inadequacy on my part, but I believe I always gave as much as I could, living my relationships to the full, just as I did the rest of my life. It hardly matters now anyway.

I worked hard, usually in my own businesses. Most were interesting, at least for a time, some were fun and a few seemed worthwhile. Usually they brought me sufficient money to be able to indulge myself. Sometimes I used my money wisely, occasionally generously, usually wastefully, to help me achieve happiness—or at least the ultimate 'good time'. I never found it of course.

My brother, David, two years older than me, lived in Paris and he *really* had money and knew how to enjoy it. He worked most of the hours of the day for many years to build up a very successful business and he thoroughly deserved and enjoyed the material and sensual diversions his success provided. An apartment in Paris, a chateaux in the countryside. a Ferrari, a yacht....

Without warning, he was dead at 42.

I had already started to realise that my life didn't seem to be going anywhere in particular but my brother's death was such a shock it prompted my re-evaluation to take on a new urgency. He and I were never really 'close' and it wasn't so much the fact of his death that shook me, it was more of the ending of his *life* and the apparent futility of everything he had done, experienced and achieved. All his success, material gains and future plans were suddenly without an iota of importance. Nor were mine.

I suppose most people ask themselves the 'why?' and 'what for?' questions at some dramatic point in their lives. Unfortunately the questions frequently seem to have no obvious answers and even if the answers are realised they may simply be too complex or frightening to acknowledge or act upon. I don't mean about death necessarily—it seems pointless to me to speculate about that—I mean about life and all its ramifications. I've never been frightened of life's ups and downs, its twists and turns, nor have I ever been frightened to actively seek to encourage change in myself. And that's what I decided to do, but I didn't really know in which direction I had to go.

By coincidence, at about that time I made my first trip to Thailand and visited many Buddhist temples. Not just the big important ones on every tourist's agenda but also little out-of-the-way 'working' monasteries. I was immensely impressed by the sense of tranquil purpose in some of them and made a point of talking at length with any English-speaking monks I could find.

I had only the most superficial understanding of what Buddhism was and much of what I thought I knew turned out to be quite wrong. I returned to England determined to find out more—though that was still mainly out of intellectual curiosity. A telephone call to the Thai Embassy put me in touch with the Thai temple in London—Wat Buddhapadipa* in Wimbledon—and soon afterwards I made the first of many hundreds of visits to that temple.

Through attending regular classes at the monastery, I learned first the basic principles of Buddhism and then something of the higher teaching and meditation. I was also lucky to meet a Thai monk there, Phra Maha Laow, who became not only my guide on many spiritual matters but also a good friend. Some years later he arranged my ordination in Bangkok.

There are two main schools of Buddhism;Theravada (Doctrine of the Elders) and Mahayana (The Great Vehicle). Theravada is considered by its adherents to be the original, orthodox Buddhism, while Mahayana is a later development and includes several schools within itself, such as Zen (itself having numerous sects). The Theravada and Mahayana schools agree on the fundamental principles of Buddhism though there are differences of emphasis on some aspects of the teaching. Most Thais are Theravadan Buddhists.

Whilst studying at Wat Buddhapadipa, I realised that Buddhism seemed to provide the answers to questions I didn't even know I had been asking myself. I also suspected that the Buddhism I had seen in Thailand had been coloured by the culture and nature of the people, and by both Animism and Brahmanism, at least at a superficial level. But that didn't really matter, nor did it affect my decision to ordain in Thailand—at that time anyway it wasn't possible to ordain in England. I decided I could be a Buddhist monk in Thailand but I didn't have to be a Thai Buddhist monk, though as it turned out this proved easier in theory than in practice.

I think I knew after only a few months of studying at Wat Buddhapadipa that I would probably ordain. It wasn't actually a difficult decision at all but it was to take nearly five years before I felt total commitment and all my circumstances came right to enable me to do so.

Eventually all my possessions were disposed of, thrown away, given away or sold and I was left literally with hardly more than the clothes I stood up in. Every time some thing left my life I found my heart a little less heavy and my mind a little more free. At that time, I moved to Wat Buddhapadipa to live as an Upasaka and helper to the temple whilst preparing for my ordination.

As an Upasaka I followed eight precepts—most lay Buddhists follow five precepts** and included in the eight were rules which helped ease me towards my forthcoming life as a monk. I could eat only before noon and then not again until the following dawn; I could not drink alcohol and I had to live a very simple lifestyle without unnecessary luxuries. I wore simple white clothes without personal adornment and cut my hair very short.

I lived full-time at the temple for about six months and they were happy days for me. As each day passed, I drew a little further away from my old lifestyle and found myself slowly beginning to understand how superficial much of my past life had been. I worked hard at the temple, helping to care for the resident monks, but also observing and learning. I learned a lot from them, but there was a great deal more I would have to learn on my own.

At last, the long-anticipated day of my departure from England came and, a little to my own surprise, there was no sense of sadness, no sense of loss and no regrets—only a great feeling of relief.

I was leaving little of importance or value behind except a few very good—and very puzzled—friends. I don't think I ever adequately explained my decision to them. One friend had asked: "Why on earth do you want to spend the rest of your life sitting cross-legged in a tropical forest watching your navel?".

I couldn't really explain but I had no doubt that I had made the right decision. I felt I had taken my first step on a new road. Quite where that road would eventually lead I had no idea.

* Wat means 'monastery' or 'temple' and Buddhapadipa means 'Light' or 'Lamp of the Buddha'.
** The Five Precepts or training rules are : 1. Not to destroy life. 2. Not to steal. 3. Not to commit adultery. 4. Not to lie. 5. Not to lose mindfulness to intoxicating drink or drugs.

Chapter 2

Why *did* I want to spend the rest of my life 'watching my navel'? I was no different from most people, but few people go to the extreme of following the path that I decided to tread. We all face much the same problems in life but frequently, I think, we find the answers in solutions that always eventually bring more of the same. Each of us would like our life to be without anguish, worry or suffering; to be fulfilled, to have meaning. We all want to be happy and we all want 'freedom'.

I believe that consciously or subconsciously we all constantly strive to change or improve our home, work and social environments to match our personal but continuously evolving ideal of what constitutes happiness and freedom.

The pressures of modern society lead many to believe that the way to happiness and freedom is through the acquisition of material things: wealth, fame, power, status, or through the accumulation of 'experiences'. But to me (now) such beliefs confuse happiness and freedom with physical well-being and personal comfort. Our ideal of happiness and freedom sometimes comes to mean the ability to fulfil our desires, to indulge ourselves; to do whatever we like within our financial and physical means.

We crave for situations and things that make us happy but when we have them, we crave for more. And we crave for release, for freedom, from that which makes us unhappy. Our conditioned clinging, craving and aversion delude our mentality, becoming the basis for habitual and frequently unwise responses to the things, people and situations with which we come into contact.

Whether we acknowledge it or not, most of us are under subtle pressure to compete, to acquire and to measure our spiritual worth by our temporal gains. We are often judged by our success or failure and may even come to judge ourselves with the same yardstick.

Some pressures are not so subtle. They assault the senses from every hoarding, from TV and radio, from every multi-coloured, flashing neon display. Bigger! Better! Newer! Try me! Buy me! And everything from washing powder to the latest model of car promises to make our lives more rewarding and more satisfying. The pressure never lets up and eventually we may come to accept that this is actually the path to happiness and contentment; that this is the 'meaning' of life. We can become so busy achieving and acquiring that we shut off that part of our intellect which might question whether this is really the right way to live our lives.

I know people do not necessarily crack under these subtle and not-so-subtle pressures, though I'm sure many do, but if we are lucky, there comes a moment when some spark of sanity inside says 'stop'. When we look around ourselves, when we stop and look within ourselves, we see that this is all basically unsatisfactory and leads nowhere—certainly not to lasting happiness, nor to true freedom. And then we may realise that we are no longer in harmony with the natural order, or with ourselves. Then perhaps we begin to wonder what it's all about, where we are going wrong—where we are *going*—and to start to search for some method to bring genuine meaning and understanding to our lives. It is at that point, I think, that many people turn to meditation.

For some it may simply be a search for a way to relax more easily, not to worry so much or to be able to cope more efficiently. For others, it may be a spiritual quest; a positive turning away from materialism and society's false values to something more deeply satisfying. Others may seek a greater understanding; for a truth that goes even beyond religious teaching.

Few people seem to know very much about meditation. Of the few, most would probably believe it is a method of relaxation that can relieve both physical and mental stress. But sitting cross-legged for half-an-hour and breathing deeply is not meditation—at best it is a relaxation therapy, at worst it is day-dreaming. If that is what is sought and if it works for the practitioner, then there is nothing wrong with it. The mind may be calmed for a short time, but stress is only temporarily relieved while the practitioner is actually doing it and perhaps for a little while afterwards. But stress is only a symptom. To remove the dis-ease entirely one must go deeper and find the cause of stress—one must go into genuine meditation.

Vipassana meditation was realised and taught by the Buddha more than 2,500 years ago. It is true Buddhist meditation and can lead to the freeing of the mind from its clinging, craving, attachment and delusion which, the Buddha taught, are the cause of all suffering and discontent. It clears the mind of all the 'mud' that has built up in it from the moment of birth leaving it, in the words of a famous Thai meditation teacher, 'Like a still forest pool'. Vipassana can lead ultimately to Insight Wisdom—personal realisation of the true nature of life, and the perfect peace that comes from that knowledge: Nibbana.

In Vipassana, Insight does not necessarily arise in a sudden flash all at once—there may be many smaller truths, many lesser insights, to be realised along the way. It takes time, patience and perseverance. Most people don't have the time and that is why the Buddha established his order of monks, so that they could withdraw from the daily pressures of lay life into an environment suitable for following the path intensely.

The Buddha described his meditation system at great length and detail in the 'Maha Satipatthana Sutta'—'The Four Foundations of Mindfulness.' Many people may know that 'watching the breath' is a Vipassana technique, but mindfulness of the breath is just one aspect of the system as a whole. The Maha Satipatthana Sutta details fourteen ways of contemplating the body, from the simple act of breathing to meditating on the nature of corpses. The Sutta also details contemplation of feelings, the activities of the mind, and mental objects.

The Buddha said in the Sutta: "This is the only way for the purification of beings, for the overcoming of sorrow and lamentation, for the destruction of suffering and grief, for reaching the right path, for the attainment of Nibbana, namely the Four Foundations of Mindfulness".

In Vipassana, the meditator 'opens up' to everything going on in the mind and body and does not deliberately exclude any thoughts, emotions or sensory perceptions that arise. The meditator does not dwell on them, nor allow them to lead to daydreaming or to discursive or judgemental thinking. They are merely observed as they arise and pass away. The meditator does not attach to any thought or emotion but merely attempts to observe dispassionately without any sense or 'I' or 'my' or 'self' being involved. Freed of the I-concept, the mind in its pure state is not disturbed by feelings such as anger, jealousy or unhappiness. It is only the I-concept which gives these feelings 'life'. Gradually the meditator begins to look at everything in a new way, unaffected by preferences, desires, craving or clinging. Eventually the level of non-attachment to thoughts and emotions increases and from this state of equanimity Insight-Wisdom (Panna) can arise.

The Venerable Sayadaw U Janaka, a Burmese meditation master, explains Vipassana in this way: 'Vipassana or Insight Meditation is, above all, experiential practice based on the systematic and balanced development of a precise and focused awareness. By observing one's moment-to-moment mind/body processes from a place of investigative attention, Insight arises into the true nature of life and experiences. Through the wisdom acquired by using Insight meditation, one is able to live more freely and relate to the world around with less clinging, fear and confusion. Thus one's life becomes increasingly directed by consideration, compassion and clarity'.

I had already practised Vipassana meditation for several years but for as long as I continued to live the lay life, with all its pressures and distractions, I knew I would never be able to progress beyond a fairly limited point. I wanted to try to go further—to reach towards the highest goals of Vipassana—and it was only by dropping out' of lay life completely that I would have the opportunity.

There are many 'states of knowledge', or insights, to be realised during Vipassana which are sometimes proceeded or accompanied by strange physical sensations or mental visions. I spend a great deal of time in meditation but as a monk never speak or write about my own experiences in any detail.

The meditation programme I had been following at Wat Buddhapadipa, and was to continue following for several more years, was that recommended in 'The Path to Nibbana' by the late Chief Meditation Master of Thailand, the Venerable Phra Dhamma Theerarach Mahamuni. Until his death in 1988, Phra Dhamma Theerarach Mahamuni was head of Section 5 at Wat Mahadhatu (pronounced Wat Mahatat) in Bangkok. He guided many thousands of students along the sometimes difficult path of Vipassana meditation. His methods were followed at Wat Buddhapadipa and many of the London-based monks had been personally trained by him.

'The Path to Nibbana' sets out a programme of 16 'Insight Meditation' exercises including walking and sitting meditation, as well as 'mindfulness' exercises. It also offers a guide to the possible 'States of Insight Knowledge' (Yanas) to be realised.

Chapter 3

As a monk I have attended dozens of ordination ceremonies in Thailand. Unfortunately the very first I attended was my own. If I had previously had the opportunity to witness the ceremony perhaps I wouldn't have been quite so nervous when my 'big day' came.

Phra Maha Laow spent many patient hours in London coaching me with the difficult Pali requests and responses that I had to make and even recorded the whole of the spoken ceremony onto cassette tape. From that, I phoneticised the Pali as closely as I could into English and typed out my 'script', including the various movements I had to make: 'Enter stage left, bow', that sort of thing.

It took me about six months to learn—a ridiculously long time compared with how quickly a Thai man can learn it and I don't think Phra Maha Laow ever understood why I felt I had to be word perfect or why I was so nervous. He kept telling me not to worry and that nobody expected me to get it 100% right. If I managed 60%, the senior officiating monk would be pleased, he said.

But Phra Maha Laow is Thai and Thai men view entering the monkhood in quite a different way from the way most Westerners do. I don't necessarily mean they take it less seriously, but as virtually every Thai man ordains at some time in his life (sometimes more than once) and as all his friends are likely to attend the ceremony, everybody eventually goes to so many ordinations that they become quite familiar with what happens. For a Westerner however, everything about the ceremony is strange: the language in which it is conducted; the traditions involved; the robes the ordainee wears before and after the ceremony; the movements and the surroundings—all are unfamiliar and daunting.

I also felt that ordaining was the most important thing I had ever done— perhaps another big difference between Thai and Western men. Even if a Thai man has only a superficial interest in Buddhism, he will still usually ordain, perhaps for a few months, or only days, to 'make merit' for his parents or because he is under great social pressure to do so. A Thai man isn't really considered 'complete' unless he has spent even a very short time in the monkhood and is sometimes referred to as 'khon dip'—an unripe person. I have even known of Thai Christians who have ordained for a short time for this reason. Temporary ordination is such an accepted tradition in Thailand that all government departments and many private companies allow up to four months 'ordination leave' for their male employees.

Of course, many Thai men ordain for a period because they seriously want to study what the Buddha taught, then they will return to their old jobs and previous lives perhaps spiritually enriched by the experience. A very few will enter the monkhood intending to stay for a short time but instead will spend the rest of their lives in the robes.

Although Thai men enter and leave the monkhood almost casually, I felt for me there would be no going back. I had given up everything to become a monk and the 'becoming' itself was such a major step that it was important to me to get it right.

Originally I had hoped to ordain at the London temple as I then thought of it as my spiritual 'home' and I knew all the monks there, but at that time it was not possible. Although the abbot of Wat Buddhapadipa was an Upachaya —a senior monk trained and authorised to conduct the ordination ceremony— Wat Buddhapadipa is a missionary temple and comes under the auspices of the Royal Thai Embassy in London, which makes it rather different from any other temple.

Each year in the summer, about a dozen young Thai boys are temporarily ordained as novice monks and live at the temple for two weeks while studying the basics of Buddhism. Many of these boys were born in England and are totally 'European-ised'. Some have never been to Thailand and some cannot speak Thai, so besides their religious training, the temporary ordination also helps them to understand something of their own cultural background. Not all the boys are willing participants in this, for even two weeks as a novice means having the head shaved. I have seen many young boys burst into tears at the sight of the razor!

Although young boys were sometimes dragged unwillingly into the Sangha, for adult men—whether European or Thai—ordination as a monk was not possible. It was decided I should ordain at Wat Mahadhatu in Bangkok because the London temple is a branch of that famous monastery. Soon after I finally left England both the abbot and the policy of Wat Buddhapadipa changed and ordination is now possible in some circumstances.

Wat Mahadhatu is a very old monastery and is also home to one of the two Buddhist universities in Thailand. There can be many hundreds of monks studying there during term time but the temple still manages to retain a wonderful air of peacefulness, despite its huge size and location at the heart of one of Bangkok's busiest tourist areas.

Phra Maha Laow was already in Thailand at Wat Mahadhatu, his 'home' temple, and I moved into Section 5 of the monastery about a week before my ordination. During that time, I had to be interviewed by the abbot to obtain his official consent. Nobody, not even a Thai man, can simply walk into a monastery and be ordained. Forms have to be filled, guarantors found and backgrounds checked. The abbot of Wat Mahadhatu, Phra Sumethadhibodi, is a very high-ranking monk indeed—he is the religious 'governor' of Bangkok province and I was (and remain) more than a little in awe of him, but he was very kind to me. Strangely, during my interview, he asked why I hadn't ordained at Wat Buddhapadipa and said he could personally see no reason why I could not have done so.

By coincidence, the abbot of Wat Buddhapadipa*and my meditation teacher, Acharn Amara Thera, were in Bangkok at that time. Phra Sumethadhibodi therefore appointed the abbot to be my Upachaya and Acharn Amara Thera as one of my two Acariyas—teachers and questioners. This considerably eased my nervousness about the coming ceremony because two of the three senior monks who would take part in the ordination already knew me well from London and would, I was sure, make some allowance for any mistakes I made. The abbot decided I should be ordained on 15th February at 9 am.

Ordination can be an expensive ceremony. Although there is no fee, it is customary in Thailand for the ordainee to offer gifts to the monks who form the Sangha which accepts him. There is a very limited number of things that can be offered and the gift usually comprises toiletries—toothpaste, tissue, soap—or similar small items. It is also customary that each monk be given a gift of money (in an envelope, so that the monk doesn't actually touch the money) with a larger amount for the Upachaya and two Acariyas. The amount offered depends entirely on the ordainee or his family's circumstances—in my experience, it may vary from 20 Baht (about 50 pence) to 100 Baht. Of course, if the family was very poor and unable to offer even a small gift, that would not prevent the ordainee from becoming a monk. The ordainee or his family must also provide a set of robes, an alms bowl and other necessities for the new monk.

There were to be 22 monks at my ordination and on my behalf Phra Maha Laow had offered lunch to about 60 others afterwards, so the expenses were going to be quite high. To my delight and amazement, a Thai lady living in London, Khun Nit, whom I had met only very briefly a few times, kindly offered to help towards the costs and even flew to Bangkok to attend the ceremony. Her generosity was to be the first of many examples of the Thai 'jai dee' — 'good heart' — that I have since encountered.

The night before a Thai man ordains is always the occasion for a big family party. Having no family in Thailand, my last evening as a layman was spent very quietly with Phra Maha Laow in his room at Wat Mahadhatu, going over the ceremony for the umpteenth time. In the final practice sessions I was word perfect. That night he shaved my head and eyebrows, which was itself an extraordinary experience.

I had been cutting my hair very short for a few months so that I would feel more accustomed to having none at all, but even so, the shock of cold water on my head when I showered afterwards was a very strange feeling. Stranger still was the image which presented itself when I looked in the mirror. The sight of my very white bald skull on top of my naturally ruddy complexion with two white gaps where my eyebrows once were seemed quite bizarre!

The practice of shaving the head is a symbolic rejection of ego and vanity. The Buddha himself, as Prince Siddhattha, cut off his own long hair soon after he left his palace and renounced his princely lifestyle. The shaving of the eyebrows is not a rule of the monks but is an old Thai tradition.

At that point, as an initiate about to enter the Sangha, I was known as a Naga which means a snake. In Buddhist legend, a snake took human shape and tried to become a monk. It was discovered and the snake was expelled from the monastery but it asked the Buddha if it could give its name to others seeking ordination. The request was granted and now all candidates for ordination are called Naga.

On the morning of my ordination I was dressed in a white sarong and a long, white, lacy robe which looked exactly like a net curtain with fancy gold trim. Usually the ordainee walks to the main monastery building—the Uposatha Hall (or Bote)—followed by his family and friends who carry his robes, alms bowl and gifts, as well as the gifts for the monks. In the absence of family, Phra Maha Laow rustled up about 20 shaven-headed and white-robed nuns from the womens' section of Wat Mahatdhatu to follow me, together with Khun Nit and members of his own family. I was very grateful for their moral support.

On our way to the Bote, we were all very surprised to meet my appointed Upachaya staggering hurriedly towards us clutching his stomach. He had suddenly been struck by a malevolent bug and was obviously in no fit state to officiate at my ceremony. He informed us that Phra Sumethadhibodi would officiate instead. In a way this was a great honour because the abbot of Wat Mahadhatu is usually too busy to undertake ordinations himself and as far as I know had never ordained a Westerner before. But all my nervousness instantly returned and I found I couldn't remember a word of the ceremony, not even my own religious name. As it turned out that didn't matter because at the very last moment the abbot decided to change my Pali name from the one I had been given at Wat Buddhapadipa to another which gave me a greater association with the London temple. I was to be Phra Peter Pannapadipo—Light, or Lamp, of Wisdom. My irrational nervousness made it a real effort to continue walking towards the Bote and I think I only managed it thanks to Phra Maha Laow's continuous "Don't worry" liturgy.

Our little procession reached the Bote and we walked around the outside three times in a clockwise direction, a symbolic way of paying respect to the 'Triple Gem'—the Buddha, the Dhamma and the Sangha. Often the ordainee is carried on the shoulders of his friends during this circumambulation, symbolising I believe Prince Siddhattha's last ride on horseback when he left his palace. At most ordinations I have attended as a monk, the followers do a lot of very loud wailing at this point, though I'm not entirely sure why. I'm glad to say that my nuns were blissfully quiet and well-behaved. I think 20 wailing nuns would just about have tipped my nerves over the edge.

Before entering the Uposatha Hall, it is a tradition in Thailand for the ordainee to turn to his followers and scatter coins, symbolising his rejection of worldly goods and materialism. I couldn't very well scatter money at the nuns since they also had rejected such things, so we skipped that tradition as well and proceeded directly into the Bote.

Inside, on a raised platform in front of a gigantic Buddha image, sat the abbot with 21 other monks ranged around him, leaving a small space for me in the middle. Phra Maha Laow was to be part of the Sangha which accepted me into its midst and he was able to sit conveniently close so that he could whisper a prompt if I stumbled over a request or a response. I approached the abbot on my knees, my package of robes resting on my forearms and my hands in a prayer-like attitude called 'anjali'. The abbot took the package from me and checked that all the necessary robes were there. I made the triple obeisance, sat back on my heels, took a deep breath and the ceremony started.

"Esaham Bhante, sucira-parinibbutampi...." "Venerable Sir, I go for Refuge to the Lord...."

Most Thai men I have seen ordained have taken the trouble to learn their lines and the correct pronunciation of the Pali, but I have seen others who haven't known a single word. As far as I recall, I don't think I did too badly. Whether that was because I actually remembered the lines or because the abbot was making allowances for me I don't know, but there is a limit to how much allowance any Upachaya will make. Every Pali word is important and must be pronounced correctly otherwise its meaning or tense may be altered. It is the Upachaya's responsibility to ensure that the ordination proceeds exactly in accordance with Sangha law and centuries-old custom.

People frequently say of personally important events that the time passed in a 'blur', or something like that. That's how it was for me. I remember entering the Bote. I remember at some point being taken aside by two monks who helped me out of my white clothes and into my saffron robes. I remember being ordered by the Upachaya to go to another part of the hall, where I was to be asked traditional questions by the two Acariyas about my health and social standing: Did I have ulcers, ringworm, consumption or epilepsy? "No, Venerable Sirs, I do not", I replied. Was I a human being? Was I a man? Was I a free man? Without debt? Exempt from government service? Did I have my parents' permission? Was I fully 20 years old? "Yes, Venerable Sirs". I remember the beautiful chanting of the monks as I poured water from a small silver jug during a ritual blessing. Lastly, I remember when my final response was made, all my lines said, and I looked at Phra Maha Laow with a great smile of relief on my face, as though to say 'I did it. I actually did it!' And he had been right of course. The whole ceremony lasted only about 50 minutes and there had been nothing to worry about at all.

Thai people love to take photographs and I was pleased to learn that someone had taken some during the ceremony. Hoping to send pictures of my 'big day' to friends in London, I ordered some prints—and was absolutely horrified when I collected them from the photo shop. In one I am bowing low before my Upachaya wearing my white net curtain. My whole body is shiny wet with nervous perspiration; my face is glowing bright red from bending and my bald, white head is gleaming and reflecting the lights of the alter candles. I looked like some hideous alien baby! Vanity prevented me from ordering reprints for my friends.

At the end of my first day as a monk, when I was alone in my tiny room in Section 5 of the monastery and was able to think clearly, I realised what an impressive ceremony I had been through. Even now, when I have been present at so many ordinations, I am still moved by the beautiful Pali requests and responses, the chanting of the monks and the traditions involved; by the feeling that this is how it has always been done and this is how it *will* always be done. And I am very glad about that. I have never seen an ordainee as nervous as I was before the ceremony, but I hope one day I will be able to guide another, perhaps a Westerner, through a similar nerve-wracking day.

I was now officially a monk and had my 'bi-suthee' my monk's identification book. With my shaven head and saffron robes I certainly looked like a monk, but now I had to begin to learn how to *be* a monk. More importantly, I had to begin ditching many of the concepts, opinions and ways of behaviour that I had collected over the previous 40 years or so on my way to this new starting point.

* At that time the abbot was Chao Khun Rachaviriyabharana but at the time of writing it was Acharn Amara Thera.

Chapter 4

One of the first problems I had to face was adjusting to monk-style accommodation. I had been told I would live in Section 5, partly because the section had some experience of Westerners and also because it had some of the best meditation teachers of any monastery in Thailand.

Section 5 is listed in many guide books as an 'international meditation centre', though I think few Westerners actually attend residential courses there. But many Thai monks come from all over the country to be taught walking and sitting meditation by the section's excellent teachers. I have also met Burmese, Sri Lankan and Korean monks there who have travelled from their own countries to learn Vipassana meditation in Thailand. Acharn Amara Thera had a permanent room in the section and both he and Phra Maha Laow thought it would be the best place for me. I had some misgivings, even though I had met the section head, Acharn Phra Maha Suparb, many times and knew him to be a kind and compassionate man.

The 24 sections of Wat Mahadhatu are built in terraces with alleys and paved areas separating the blocks. Each section has a senior monk as its head and most are home to at least five or six monks—sometimes many more—a couple of novices, several temple boys and an assortment of cats and dogs. In the Pansa, or Rains Retreat, when many Thai men ordain for a few months, the sections can be considerably more crowded.

Most of the single-storey terraced buildings were originally exactly the same but they had all been altered and added to by generations of section heads. Each reflected the style and resources of its past and present residents, exactly as a row of Victorian terraced houses does in England. Inside, some were rather like run-down but pretty Spanish villas, with terracotta floors and stucco walls; some were filled with orchids and other tropical plants: some were well-kept and clean and others were gloomy rat-infested hovels. At that time Section 5 fell into the last category, though it has since been repainted from top to bottom and is now a much more pleasant environment.

The section had originally been the same type of building as most of the others but over many years had been adapted and added to in a seemingly haphazard manner. Some monk rooms on the original ground floor of the building were large and airy, others in two additional floors that had been added to the roof were not. The rooms at the very top were tiny, about seven foot square, and although some had windows that opened onto fresh air, others were in dark and stuffy corridors. Section 5 was unusual in that it had a separate section within itself for nuns, and taking into account resident monks, visiting monks, novices, nuns and temple boys, the section's residents probably numbered 40 or 50. It seemed very crowded to me but many monks had lived there for years and seemed perfectly happy to call it home.

At first I was allocated one of the tiny inner rooms on the top floor and my window opened onto a partially enclosed space through which no breeze, let alone air, ever seemed to flow. The room had a fan but in such a small area it just seemed to move the stifling air around without actually cooling it at all.

I had always had space in my life, lots of it. I am not claustrophobic but I needed space. All my flats or houses had been large and my last in London was a three-storey, three-bedroomed house in which I lived alone. I liked space; clean, white, empty space, and had only ever owned the minimum of furniture that I actually needed. Even my furniture had to be 100% functional—'minimalist' I believe it was called. My friends used to say that visiting my home was like visiting a clinic, it was so stark and antiseptic but I had never been able to relax fully in a cluttered room. I would quickly become agitated by the clutter, by ornaments, 'knick knacks' and by unnecessary visual distractions. I wasn't one of those neatness freaks who wanted to tidy up other people's homes when I visited, other people could have as much clutter as they liked, but I wanted none of it.

Well, my room in Section 5 was about as minimalist as it is possible to be. It certainly had no clutter. Apart from the fan, it had a plastic mat, a bare fluorescent tube and a large number of ants. But it also had precious little space. I couldn't see any way I could adjust to living there: it was smaller than the toilet in my last house. "Too small, too stuffy, too....", I whined to Phra Maha Laow, but I had no choice. This was the room I had been allocated, this was where I had to live. I was just going to have to start the difficult process of adjusting my rigid ideas about what I believed I needed or had to have. Not just about my 'space', but about many other things too.

I had thought for more than four years about becoming a monk, but sitting in that tiny room some of the realities of my new life started to hit me. I began to wonder whether I had given too much thought to the potential spiritual benefits and not enough to the practicalities, the hardships and the discipline I would have to face. But I knew they were directly related and each led to, or helped support the other. My thoughts were confused and I started my first night as a monk in a miserable, depressed mood.

I had been lucky enough in the past to have travelled extensively, sometimes staying for fairly long periods in exotic lands, and I had never once felt homesick. But then I had always known that whatever adventures, difficulties or hardships I encountered on my travels, 'home' was always there, just a few hours flying time away. I could always return home, full of tales and experiences to relate to my friends, and I could resume my old lifestyle again.

My old lifestyle.... a night out at the theatre or cinema, a wild party, long drives through the English countryside in an open-topped sports car, racing down to the coast on a big motorcycle late at night just for the hell of it, eating good food in expensive restaurants with a bottle or two of fine wine, curling up on my settee in front of the telly with a hot and spicy pizza in a warm cardboard box on my lap, shopping in London's West End, knowing I could buy anything with a flash of gold plastic, or deluding myself for a few hours that *this* time, with *this* person, it was the 'Real Thing'.

It was all gone now and could never be regained. I had made sure of that. The smoke from my social and financial burning bridges could be smelt from London to Bangkok. Almost from the moment, years before, when I had decided that one day I would ordain, I had deliberately started to cut myself off from it all. But now, today, was the day; the day when I finally had to face the fact: there was no going back. That period of my life had ended utterly.

I had never experienced such feelings of great loss or uncertainty before and a part of me still clung to that past. Not, I think, because I had actually enjoyed any of it so much, but because it was what I had always known; it was *all* I had known. It was my life and I could cope with it. Now I was facing a new and totally different lifestyle, much of it completely strange to me. On that first evening I was, I think, a little scared. Lonely too.

But although my future lifestyle was largely unsure, one thing that was already known was that which had brought me to this strange new starting point: the teaching of the Buddha. In the Dhamma I could find all the strength and inspiration I needed to face whatever lay ahead of me.

I sat on the vinyl floor for a long time feeling quite dejected. Then I looked at my small pile of possessions—a couple of extra robes, my alms bowl, a few books and very little else and I realised this was everything in the world that I owned, needed or wanted. Well, they didn't take up much space and what was this room for anyway? It was a place to sleep in, eat in, to study and to meditate in. None of those activities required vast expanses of floor, interesting angles or exciting lighting. There was, in fact, ample space for what I needed to do.

Luckily for me, after a few weeks, a corner room on the top floor became empty and I was able to move from my inner corridor. Although my new room was just as tiny, it had the advantage of an extra window and both windows opened out into fresh air and I had a pleasant view across the monastery's colourfully-tiled rooftops.

I rather surprised myself by adjusting fairly quickly and painlessly to my restricted living area, though then it was adjustment caused by necessity. It was some considerable time later, after I had stayed in different monasteries and lived in a variety of rooms or kutis that I believe I really adjusted and started to become detached from such concerns. I realised that space, or the lack of it, in fact my whole personal environment, had ceased to bother me. The longer I remained a monk, the more uncluttered my mind became. It took quite a time but my mind slowly began to develop its own space and a freedom that was confined neither by walls nor by preconceived ideas.

As I write these notes, I am sitting in the bedroom of my present kuti, though it doesn't actually have a bed. It is a large, old and typically Thai-style wooden house perched on stilts, with polished wooden floors and many shuttered windows. It has three rooms and I live alone, though I would welcome any other monk who wished to live here. Pots of colourful plants sit on the large balcony and there are cats everywhere, basking in the sun. It is quite charming and I am content to be here, but I know I could move tomorrow to a box room without a second thought. Any small possessions I have gathered or been given by lay-people will stay on here, a gift for the next occupant.

When I occasionally need to go to Bangkok, I stay at Wat Mahadhatu in Section 5. It's OK. Sometimes I am allocated a large room, sometimes a small one, but it's all the same really. Where I am is home and I carry my space with me wherever I go.

Chapter 5

The first thing any new monk needs to know is how to dress himself. I had exchanged clothes kept up and held together by zips, belts, buttons, press-studs and Velcro for a large rectangle of cotton and unless it was actually tied in a knot somewhere, I couldn't see how it could stay on. Often mine didn't. It didn't only fall off, it actually seemed to leap off me.

I was familiar with monks' robes from my years at the London temple and had often seen monks wrap themselves in their outer robes, but it always seemed to be done so quickly that I still hadn't a clue how to do it myself. Of course, I had never had the opportunity to wear one before — I think any monk would be genuinely horrified if a layman put on the robes, even for practice, before being properly ordained.

In modern times, the monk's wardrobe consists of his outer robe civara (jivorn) and an under-robe antaravassaka (sabong) that is worn around the waist, covering the navel and falling to just below the knees. The sabong is held up by a fold and a tuck and a cord belt. On the top part of his body, under the jivorn, is worn a sort of sleeveless one-shouldered waistcoat (ungsa) which is joined together on the left side by tying tags. For religious services inside the monastery, the monk also wears an additional robe (sanghati) which is folded in a very particular way into a long rectangle and hung over the left shoulder.

The monk may or may not wear sandals, depending on the tradition of his particular monastery, though most do. He may carry a soft bag, called a yarm, which is like a shoulder bag but which is carried in the crook of the arm and should never be worn on the shoulder or slung over the back.

The robes come in different sizes and nowadays are usually made of cotton, silk, nylon or some other man-made fabric, but they are always cut to the same pattern and design. They are actually made from many pieces of cloth sewn together in, according to legend, the pattern of the paddy fields of Magadha in Northern India. They are made in many pieces to recall the days when monks made their own robes from bits of cloth found in charnel grounds.

The size and way of wearing the outer robe has changed since the Buddha's time and may vary a little from country to country, but however it is worn, the monk should always look neat and his body should be well covered.

In Thailand the jivorn is large and is generally wrapped around the body with the two ends rolled together. This roll is taken over the left shoulder and under the left arm so that its end can be held in the left hand or pressed firmly between the arm and the body. Inside the temple the robe is worn so that the right shoulder is exposed, but outside the temple both shoulders and arms are covered. The colour of the robes varies from monastery to monastery—at Wat Mahadhatu they are a reddish-brown but at others may be anything from very dark brown to brilliant yellow, or even 'day-glo' orange.

On the morning after my ordination I got up at 5 am and tried to dress myself in my outer robe in preparation for breakfast in the section. Then I tried again. And again. The breakfast bell rang and still I seemed to have either too much robe left over or not enough. Chanting from the dining hall signalled the end of breakfast and by then I was in an absolute sweat and still looked like a sack of potatoes, with lumps and bumps and bunches of cloth exactly where they shouldn't have been. One moment the bottom of the robe was at knee height, the next flapping around my ankles. Wrapping the outer robe is actually not a difficult task—once you know how—but I didn't know and I found myself getting intensely irritated. Each time I tried to wrap the jivorn it looked worse than the last time. Even in the early morning my tiny room was stiflingly warm and both my robe and I were wet with sweat. I was quite close to tears of anger and frustration. "Calm down, calm down" I told myself repeatedly.

One of the problems was that I am six feet tall and the ceiling of my room was only inches more. To get a neat roll of cloth to pass over my shoulder, I needed to raise my left arm quite high while rolling the ends of the cloth together. As my room was on the top floor, I eventually clambered out onto the roof, where I had sufficient space to get the robe wrapped around me in something vaguely approaching the correct way, but only very vaguely. I looked a mess and the pigeons were not impressed. Phra Maha Laow's room was in Section 24 at the other end of the monastery, but I managed the distance without anything falling off and he was able to dress me neatly in seconds, as well as offering me his breakfast 'left overs'.

I think my biggest fear as a new monk was of my under-robe falling down in the street. The sabong is held up by a one and a half inch-wide woven belt with two very long cords. The belt and cords are passed around the waist twice and the cords are tied in a bow at the front. The cords are a bit like over-sized versions of round, nylon shoe laces, which I never found stayed tied together as well as the old, flat cotton type. Many monks, including me, wear a key ring at the end of one of the cords and if the ring has several keys on it, they make that end quite a bit heavier than the other—enough to gradually pull a poorly-tied bow undone.

In my first month as a monk, this happened to me as I was descending a very rickety staircase, when for safety I needed to support myself with both arms outstretched. As I came down, I felt an unusual movement under my jivorn and was horrified when my belt slipped down past my knees and around my feet. I knew the sabong wouldn't be long after and it wasn't. I couldn't make a grab for it because I would quite likely have fallen down the stairs, which would have been even less impressive to the group of Thai people who were waiting at the bottom to come up. I sort of hopped out of my sabong, calmly gathered it up, put it in my yarm and walked away with as much dignity as I could salvage. But at least I didn't expose myself to total ridicule as I did on another occasion.

At that time, I was living in a remote country monastery and had to shift some very large rocks. Being in an isolated part of the grounds and as I was working alone, I had taken off my outer robe and ungsa, just leaving my sabong wrapped around me. Staggering under the weight of a huge boulder, with my body arched backwards, I didn't notice that my belt had come adrift—until my sabong started to slide down my legs. There's not a lot one can do when both hands are full of boulder and before I could drop the rock, my sabong was around my ankles, leaving me totally naked (except, perversely, for the belt, which was still hanging loosely around my waist). I had *thought* I was alone but loud screams of delighted laughter from behind a bush told me that, as usual, some of the village children had come to see what the strange foreign monk was up to. After that, I started to tie my belt so tightly I often gave myself stomach ache!

I'm not sure at what point dressing myself neatly and securely became second nature, but of course it did eventually and now I can't see why I ever thought it was such a problem. I had to learn to dress myself and learn many other practical daily matters as soon as I could, because Phra Maha Laow was due to return to London a few weeks after my ordination. He devoted endless hours in trying to teach me not only how to dress but also how to walk in the robes, how to sit on the floor, change position, get up, how to make a triple bow to a senior monk and so on.

I had already picked up a lot of tips simply from watching the monks at Wat Buddhapadipa, but there was a great deal more I hadn't noticed nor even thought about. Many Thai men, especially in rural areas, wear little other than a sarong for much of the time and many of their daily activities are done at floor level. They know instinctively how to make these movements neatly, politely and modestly. But I have also seen 'city bred' new monks who don't, and they are frequently as immodest as I sometimes was.

Just about every aspect of the monks' behaviour is governed by the Vinaya—the 227 training rules—many of which were laid down by the Buddha himself. They include almost every daily action and it is very necessary for a monk to know all these rules and to understand the reasons for them. At the time of my ordination, I knew the most important rules but there were many other 'minor' ones and even more Thai traditional rules and customs that I didn't know.

It is especially important for a Western monk to be aware of the training rules and he must be constantly mindful of his public behaviour and deportment. A Thai monk walking too quickly in the street, or swinging his arms as he walked, would probably go unnoticed by most Thai people simply because there are so many Thai monks. But a Western monk is such an unusual sight anywhere in Thailand that his every movement is watched with great interest and he is more likely to be remarked upon than is his Thai counterpart.

I remember Phra Maha Laow once told me that if there were two monks sitting on a bench, one Thai and one Western, and both were smoking cigarettes, a Thai observer would be quite shocked by the Westerner, but probably wouldn't even notice that the Thai monk was also smoking.*

So, my education and training were to be fairly intensive for the first few weeks and Phra Maha Laow would not allow me to go outside the temple until he felt I would be able to conduct myself in public reasonably well.

Even though I am usually a very shy person, I was desperate to walk in the streets as a monk and show myself off. This was pure vanity of course and I knew it even then, but I had to start learning to be patient.

Happily, after a few days, Phra Maha Laow decided that I was probably able to behave myself reasonably well and he suggested we should visit Wat Phra Kaew, the Temple of The Emerald Buddha, which is only a short walk from Wat Mahadhatu.

With my robe properly arranged for walking outside, my totally empty yarm placed on my left arm, and my new and somewhat less-than-stylish plastic sandals with the irritating squeak doused with water to quieten them down a bit, we walked to the gates of Wat Mahadhatu. I was tremendously and unreasonably excited about my first 'public appearance' though of course I could not let my excitement show. Phra Maha Laow had instructed me that I must walk slowly, calmly, with eyes downcast, being careful not to brush up against anybody. "But Phra Maha Laow, how can I avoid brushing up against people if I'm looking at the pavement?", I asked. "Don't worry", he said, "They'll see you".

And see me they did. We must, I suppose, have presented a curious spectacle. Phra Maha Laow is very short, even for a Thai, and I tower over him. It is actually quite impolite in Thai society and especially in Thai monk society, for a junior to have his head higher than that of his senior, but there was little I could do about that except to walk a few paces behind him.

Unfortunately being tall I also have a problem about walking slowly. It's not that I walk fast, but my legs are so long that I take huge strides. I tried to walk more slowly by shortening my strides but I found this quite awkward and ungainly, so Phra Maha Laow was constantly whispering to me to slow down as I was frequently close to overtaking him.

Almost the instant we stepped over the threshold of Wat Mahadhatu, I heard someone say "Phra Farang"—foreign monk. The first of dozens of times that day and the first of many hundreds of thousands of times since. Phra Farang ... Phra Farang ... Phra Farang. Even many Thai People who know me quite well, frequently refer to me as Phra Farang rather than as Phra Peter and I have never understood why, not that I care really. I know that many Westerners who visit Thailand feel quite insulted when they are referred to as 'farang', though the Thai people rarely use the word in an insulting way. I have been told by a linguist that Westerners may find the word insulting because it has two syllables, like many of the racially insulting words or taunts that are used in the West. But I wasn't insulted, I was proud to be a Phra Farang. As we walked people smiled at me. I smiled back. In fact I positively beamed until a warning glance from my teacher made me lower my eyes and fix a more neutral expression on my face. But I couldn't keep my eyes downcast for long, not with so many lovely Thai smiles being offered to me.

We certainly didn't have to worry about brushing up against anybody for although the area around Wat Mahadhatu was at that time a market and the footpath was crowded, the crowds simply parted to let us through. "Phra Farang.....Phra Farang.....Phra Farang".

Besides smiling, many people also offered me a very graceful wai as we passed — a lovely Thai gesture of both greeting and respect, in which the palms are held together as if in prayer and the finger tips brought up level with the nose.

Of course, my vanity and ego were so inflated by all this that at the time I didn't realise I might just as well have been carrying a big placard saying 'brand new monk'. My head was newly-shaved and shining brightly, whereas Phra Maha Laow's black hair had grown noticeably since the last general head-shaving day two weeks before. My robes still had their brand new sheen and creases, like an unironed new shirt, and although I tried to walk like a monk, it must have been obvious from the way I kept having to hitch my robe onto my shoulder, and my whole general demeanour, that I was new at all this. That didn't stop people smiling or wai-ing of course, for in my experience, Thai people are usually genuinely delighted that a Westerner has chosen to follow Buddhism and has become a monk in their country, even though they often don't understand why.

But a monk like Phra Maha Laow, with more than 15 years spent in the robes, has developed an air of serenity that cannot be falsified. It cannot really even be learned — it is a reflection of true inner peace and comes from a genuine understanding of what the

Buddha taught and from long practise of Buddhist meditation techniques. Thai people seem to instinctively recognise this natural serenity and I didn't have it.

None of that occurred to me at the time. There I was, in my lovely new robes and my lovely new hair cut, walking on the streets of Bangkok while total strangers smiled and paid their respects to me. Oh, I was the bee's knees!

But not for long......

* A 1994 report in, I think, the *Bangkok Post* said that 85% of monks outside of Bangkok smoke, but there is no specific rule preventing smoking.

Chapter 6

For me, Wat Phra Kaew ranks as one of the most beautiful and fantastic religious monuments on earth. Compared with most other such man-made monuments, Wat Phra Kaew is 'new', most of it dating back only about 200 years. But as an example of inspired architecture, of man's desire to revere his gods or spiritual leaders, the Temple of The Emerald Buddha is truly remarkable.

Golden pagodas gleam in the sun, soaring pillars and columns are covered with millions of tiny pieces of coloured glass and porcelain which glitter and sparkle, dazzling the eyes. Mythological giants and heavenly creatures stand guard at the gates and every surface is carved, coloured or embellished. The tourists and visitors who throng its courtyards are always quiet, perhaps stunned by the vibrant beauty and brilliant colour that surrounds them.

The origins of the image known as The Emerald Buddha are shrouded in mystery. In 1434 it was found hidden in an old chedi in Chiang Rai in the north of Thailand, disguised with plaster and gold leaf. It was enshrined in various temples in the north and later in Laos. In 1778, Chao Phraya Chakri, later to become Rama I, the founder of the present royal dynasty, brought the image back to Thailand, to Thonburi, then the capital. The image made its final move in 1785, when Bangkok was established as the new capital and the Chapel Royal was built.

The image is really quite small, about 60 centimetres high, and it is not made of emerald but of jade or jasper. Some historians believe the image is of Thai workmanship, possibly from the Chiang Sen period (about 1050 AD) and that the material used probably came from Southern China. Other historians believe the image came from India.

What it is made of or where it originated is unimportant compared to its meaning to the Thai people. It has become a talisman of the people, the religion, the nation and its sovereign. It is said that if the image should ever leave Bangkok, the 200-year-old Chakri dynasty will fall. The Chakri kings traditionally anoint the image and change its robes three times each year, at the beginning of the three Thai seasons. The robes themselves are very beautiful. The rainy season robe is of gold decorated with rubies, with a gold and sapphire head-dress. The cool season robe is covered in gold beads and that for the hot season includes a crown of gold, and jewelled ornaments that almost cover the image. Great power is attributed to The Emerald Buddha. During a cholera outbreak in Bangkok in 1820, the image was carried through the streets of the city in an attempt to end the spread of the disease. People travel from all over the country to pay respect to the image and to 'pray' for some favour or relief from illness.

Nobody except the King may even approach the image and it sits very high up on a pedestal, protected by a glass case, barriers and vigilant guards. It is also one of the very few Buddha images in Thailand that may not be photographed. I have frequently seen the guards exposing film of clandestine photography, usually very much to the tourists' annoyance despite the fact that there are 'no photography' signs.

I do not 'worship' Buddha images. I respect them all, large or small, new or old, because they are symbolic representations of the founder of my religion and for me, that symbolism includes everything that I believe and try to follow and practise. I sometimes use a small Buddha image to focus my mind before meditation and I happily and humbly bow before the main image in any monastery I visit. This is a personal reaffirmation of my beliefs, but I do not believe any image is 'holy', nor even ultimately important, nor do I accept that any image or 'holy relic' can have magical powers. But I could be quite wrong and I am sure most Thais would say I am, and most certainly where The Emerald Buddha is concerned.

From the moment I first saw The Emerald Buddha many years ago on my first visit to Thailand, I had been enthralled by this lovely object. On every opportunity when in Bangkok, I always spent a half hour or so sitting in the Chapel Royal staring up at the image and its surrounding alter decorations. Like any other visitor, I could not get very close. The only people who are allowed to pass the barriers are monks who come to pay their respects. Now I was to be allowed that privilege.

Before, when I had visited Wat Phra Kaew and the adjoining Grand Palace, I had had to queue with other tourists to buy a ticket. Like many other 'attractions' in Thailand, Wat Phra Kaew has a two-tier pricing system: tourists pay, Thais don't. In the case of The Emerald Buddha I think that's quite fair but on this occasion, my first visit as a monk, I wondered what my position would be. Would I have to queue and pay or would I be allowed through the 'Thais only' gate? I was waved through with a wai and a smile and, for the first time, heard the phrase "Nimmon Luang Por"—"Invite Respected Father". My vanity meter quivered, not sure whether to move up or down a point.

Inside we wandered around for a while, studying the recently restored mural paintings depicting scenes from the Ramakien, the Thai version of India's Ramayana. I was aware that we seemed to have gathered quite a crowd of people behind us, a few Thais but mostly tourists, who followed us quietly from panel to panel. We decided to sit for a while in a small open-sided pavilion but as soon as we sat down we were surrounded by people, all pointing cameras and camcorders at us. Dozens of them. A Japanese gentleman sat next to me while his companion took photographs. Then a couple of Germans, then an American. I expected that at any moment, somebody would sit on my lap to pose with me, or plonk a 'kiss me quick' hat on my head, just for a laugh. I found myself intensely irritated, though I tried hard not to let it show. People were pointing their cameras at us as though we were just another tourist attraction, something to be photographed to show the folks back home. We were Buddhist monks, wearing the robes of that ancient order, but we might just as well have been wearing Mickey Mouse costumes for the benefit of visitors to Disneyland.

I personally felt insulted because I thought people showed not the slightest degree of good manners, but I was also irritated at a deeper level because somehow the robe and everything it symbolised seemed diminished by this intrusion. I was appalled and deeply embarrassed. Phra Maha Laow seemed oblivious to all this and sat, smiling calmly.

I asked Phra Maha Laow if we could move on. We started walking towards the Chapel Royal, followed by our gaggle of tourists and preceded by others a few feet in front walking backwards and keeping their camcorders fixed on our faces. Mine, I think, was bright red. A few yards from the hall, two young Englishmen, probably in their mid-20s, sidled up to me and politely asked: "Why are you a monk?". I replied that I had become a monk because I wanted to devote my life to following what the Buddha taught. "You look like a bloody idiot", said one and they walked off, laughing.

I was trembling when we entered the Chapel and a guard led us through the assembly of about a hundred people, Thais and tourists, who were sitting on the floor. Now there is a screen between the main floor of the hall and the area reserved for monks, but at that time there was only an open barrier and the monks could be seen at their devotions. We sat in silent thought for a few minutes—mine quite different from Phra Maha Laow's I'm sure, and then began to make the triple obeisance. My robe fell off.

I actually felt quite faint and nauseous and it was only with great effort that I got up and walked with any dignity at all through the crowd and into the sunshine. Outside we again found ourselves the focus of every camera and camcorder and though I smiled, inwardly I was cringing with humiliation.

"Phra Farang....Phra Farang... Bloody idiot."

When we got back to Wat Mahadhatu, I tried to explain my feelings to Phra Maha Laow, though I was confused and didn't really understand them myself. I felt I had been personally insulted by the two boys and I thought the robes and what they symbolised had been degraded by the tourists.

"You shouldn't worry", said Phra Maha Laow. I don't know how many times I have heard my friend and teacher say "Don't worry" during our long relationship. It's his answer to most problems. In the West we say it, but I don't think we really know what it means or how to do it. It's about as valid as "You should pull your socks up". We know it's good advice, often the only advice, but we do worry; some of us all the time, about every little thing. And that worry can lead to the most awful inner turmoil and suffering. Worrying *at* a problem may help unravel it and maybe a solution will present itself, but worrying *about* it will only ever make it worse. But when Phra Maha Laow used the term, "Don't worry" or that most famous of Thai phrases, 'Mai bpen rai' — 'It doesn't matter' — he really meant it. He doesn't worry. It doesn't matter. He seems to manage to keep both an inner and outer equanimity at all times and that was something I had not learned to do. I had no natural sense of 'Mai bpen rai' or if I'd ever had it, it had long ago been buried under layers of personal opinion, and habitual, conditioned responses: "*I* think it matters"... "It matters to *me*"... "in *my* opinion... " — all just ego.

Phra Maha Laow said that if someone had shown impoliteness to me, either verbally or through their actions, it could only affect me and disturb my equanimity if I allowed it to. Possibly Westerners are more aggressive than Thai people. If someone insults us, our egos and our pride may be offended and perhaps we feel the need to respond in kind. This is not really the Thai way and it certainly shouldn't be the monks' way — and it doesn't lead to inner tranquillity.

I remember at one of my very first lessons in Buddhism at Wat Buddhapadipa, being told by the monk-teacher: "If you are playing tennis and someone hits the ball at you, there are two choices—you can either catch it or hit it back". Although he may have been a little confused about the rules of tennis, there was obvious wisdom in what he was trying to say. If you don't respond to an insult in any way—if the mind doesn't move—the insult does not exist. An insult is only the opinion of someone else, who quite likely doesn't have any facts upon which to base that opinion; he is simply sounding off for some unrelated reason of his own and the words therefore have no validity. So why should the mind move? And if there is no ego, no vanity, there is nothing that can be hurt or offended anyway.

I think on that day, only a few days after my ordination, I had my first real lesson about the false nature of ego and pride—something which I may have absorbed intellectually from studying at Wat Buddhapadipa but which I didn't know experientially.

When walking to Wat Phra Kaew, I had been proud to be a monk, to show myself off to the people and to accept their 'wais' and respect. But they knew nothing about *me*. The tourists offered no 'wais' or respect because they also didn't know who I was or what I represented. One group of people thought I looked like somebody deserving of respect and another thought I looked like 'a bloody idiot'. Both opinions were based solely on what I was wearing and my physical appearance. Ultimately neither opinion had any validity, but I had allowed pride and ego to respond to both in different ways.

Inner equanimity is a state of mind which is not disturbed by outside stimuli. The mind is not disturbed by words, no matter whether they are insulting or flattering. All stimuli, regardless of whether they come by ear, eye, nose, touch or taste are regarded with absolute tranquillity. Equanimity comes from a true understanding of what the Buddha taught—not at an intellectual level but from really *knowing* for oneself. But it doesn't come easily and I was to have more humiliating experiences in the future, before I even began to know equanimity sufficiently enough to wrap it around myself as naturally as my robe.

Eventually I began to see my robe in quite a different way also. I saw it for what it was intended to be—a cloth to keep my body covered and as a protection from insects and the elements. It had symbolic significance as well, but that was something that had grown up incidentally around it. The robe could neither be insulted, nor flattered. It was just a piece of cloth. Only I and my preconceptions and misconceptions could be insulted, and only if I allowed my mind to respond.

Since that first visit as a monk to Wat Phra Kaew, I have returned many times. The tourists and visitors are still there of course, with their cameras and camcorders. Some are very polite and occasionally ask if they may take my photograph, which I never refuse. Some want to spend a few minutes discussing Buddhism, or more likely, why an Englishman should want to become a monk. Some don't ask before sticking their lenses in my face and very rarely someone will surprise me by making some insulting taunt or disparaging remark, but these are usually about my physical appearance rather than my religion and some of the insults are witty and clever. My robe no longer falls off when I make the triple obeisance before The Emerald Buddha and if it did, I wouldn't worry. I'd straighten it up and put it back on. But that's now.

Chapter 7

When I made my first visit to Thailand I had sent postcards to friends in England showing monks on their early morning almsround — going out on binderbaht. The image of the line of shaven-headed, saffron-robed monks was so exotic and so evocative of the country that I wanted my friends to see it too. Not that I actually saw monks on binderbaht myself — I was never out of my hotel bed early enough for that. But even the postcard photographs seemed to hint that far from being what I then vaguely thought of as 'beggars', the monks had a nobility about them and that the custom was of great religious significance. Now I was a member of their community I was excited by the prospect of taking part in the daily ceremony myself.

First of course I had to be trained and Phra Maha Laow was certainly not going to let me loose on the good people of Bangkok until he was confident I knew how to go out on binderbaht properly.

The Buddha went on almsround and although the robes and alms-bowl have changed over the centuries it is still done in essentially the same way. The Vinaya includes many training rules about the conduct of the monk whilst on binderbaht. In modern times, it is not always possible to follow some of the rules to the letter, but monks must try to follow the spirit of the Vinaya as closely as they can.

For example, the training rules say that the monk may accept food (ie. curries, etc.) in the proportion of 1 to 4 of rice; he can accept food only up to the edge of his alms-bowl and he must not hide curries under the rice in order to get more. But the nature of food itself has changed since these and other rules were laid down in India so many centuries ago. Now, at least in the towns and cities of Thailand, food offered to the monks is often in packets, bottles and cans and even the rice may be in a bag or polystyrene box.

Thai people love to offer food to the monks since they believe they 'make merit' by doing so. Frequently it is impossible to accept only a level bowl full and many monks carry a yarm or plastic carrier bag in which to put the excess they are offered. To refuse food, thus refusing to allow the people to 'make merit', would be considered extremely rude. So monks must compromise as necessary but still try to go out on binderbaht according to the ancient traditions. The excess food I usually collected was no problem for me because I shared my food with the nuns in Section 5, who of course did not go out on binderbaht

At most city temples, the monks go out on binderbaht alone or in very small groups and it is usually only in rural areas that all the monks from the village temple go out on binderbaht together. Not all monks go out on binderbaht every day, though I think the majority do. In Section 5 of Wat Mahadhatu the temple boys cooked a simple breakfast every morning for the monks who for whatever reason were unable to go out 'on their rounds'. In other sections some monks went on binderbaht and then shared their collected food with others in the section, perhaps on some sort of rota basis. In European and American Thai Buddhist temples the monks do not go out on binderbaht at all because they live within cultures which are unfamiliar with Buddhism or the tradition of going out on binderbaht.

For my first few days as a monk I ate breakfast in Section 5, together with a monk with a broken leg, a couple of visiting Korean monks and others who had various early morning duties. On about the fourth day Phra Maha Laow decided that we would go out on binderbaht together.

That was to be only the second time I had stepped out of the monastery gates as a monk and I was looking forward not only to learning how to go out on binderbaht but also to the walk on Bangkok's pre-dawn streets. We were back within 10 minutes, our bowls full. "I want to go again", I said. He was shocked. "You can only go out on binderbaht once". "It wasn't long enough". "You can only go out on binderbaht once". "I didn't learn anything..." Phra Maha Laow and I were well-known at Wat Buddhapadipa for the frequency and futility of our arguments. He usually knew what was right and I always knew what I wanted. Usually he won, but on this occasion he gave in. We dropped off our first load of food at his section. "We're like naughty novices" he said, as we stepped through the gates for the second time.

In fact the practicalities of going out on binderbaht are simple and I learned quickly how to walk, stand, hold my bowl and accept food. There hadn't been time to dwell on the significance of any of it and it was not until the next day, when I went out alone, that I understood *what* I was doing. My teacher had been unable to prepare me for the spiritual and cultural shock I was about to receive.

Spiritual experience was the last thing on my mind next morning as I prepared to leave the monastery and take to the streets. My main concern was keeping a firm grip on my bowl and holding it level. Modern bowls are large, I believe much larger than in the Buddha's time, and they can be awkward to handle, especially when someone puts a bag or spoonful of very hot rice in them. The heat of the rice is transmitted immediately through the bowl to the hands and I have sometimes been scorched by the hot metal. Modern bowls are often made of stainless steel with a very thin and light-weight tin lid. This fits only loosely on top of the bowl and is quite likely to fall off with a loud and embarrassing clatter if the bowl is tipped at the wrong angle. I was still having a problem keeping my robe on too. It was fine if I stood still with the roll of cloth that holds it together tucked tightly under my arm, but as soon as I made any sort of movement the robe would shift on my shoulders and threaten to fall in a heap around me.

As I stood bare-footed at the gate of Wat Mahadhatu, my main thoughts were with these practical matters, as well as the state of the pavements outside. The vicinity of any temple in Bangkok is home to countless stray dogs, since even the mangiest mutt is sure of a meal in the temple and they leave evidence of their presence every few yards. Bangkok's pavements are themselves dangerous, with holes big enough and deep enough to break a leg in, but stepping off the pavement to walk in the road brings its own dangers. Slimy vegetables from yesterday's market fill the gutters, just waiting to be trodden on—banana skins in the most literal sense. I had all these potential hazards in mind as I prepared to step through the gate. And of course I was nervous.

There is a form of meditation which focuses concentration on very precise movements of the feet and I decided to calm my nerves by treating binderbaht as a meditation exercise. After adjusting my robe one last time and clutching my bowl tightly with two hands to my stomach, I took a deep breath and stepped over the temple threshold.

I had decided to go on a less populated route for my first binderbaht alone so that I could be out longer. My route was to take me around Wat Mahadhatu, past Wat Phra Kaew and to a small market about a kilometre away.

I have never experienced anything in my life like that 45-minute walk. I had intended practising only the simplest walking meditation—concentrating on each foot as it was moved forward—*right goes thus, left goes thus*—but my concentration level quickly became so high that it soon encompassed my whole body. For the first time, I really understood 'walking' and each step seemed to be a unique experience. I was aware of the movement of every leg and foot muscle; aware of my own weight as each foot touched the ground; the texture and dampness of the surface I was walking on; the cool air on my shaven head, the feel and weight of the bowl in my hands; everything seemed to take on a new reality. In fact, I was so absorbed in my meditation I wasn't aware of the first layperson waiting to offer food and walked straight past her!

The ceremony of offering food is simple but full of symbolism. The layperson waits at the side of the road with a basket or tray of food, usually rice and curries packed in little plastic bags, a piece of fruit, perhaps some cake or other sweet, and occasionally a 10 or 20 Baht note in an envelope. The monk approaches with eyes downcast, looking only at the pavement, mindful of every step. As the monk draws nearer, the layperson invites him to accept food. Monks do not beg. Laypeople invite him to accept their offerings by saying "Nimmon". Without looking up, the monk stops walking and stands quietly still. These few moments of complete stillness enable the donor to consider the merit of his or her action and the monk to contemplate the meaning of the food which is about to be offered. Then, bending forward very slightly from the waist, the monk raises the lid of his bowl and the donor gently places the food inside. The monk should not look at the donor but keeps his attention on the bowl. The donor pays respect to the monk with a graceful 'wai'; the lid of the bowl is lowered and the monk walks on his way. The monk should never say 'Thank you' but occasionally may murmur a very short blessing. Usually no words are spoken and none are necessary, for both monk and layperson are aware that they have followed a tradition which has barely changed in thousands of years.

To me this was not only beautiful but also quite surreal. I was a 45-year-old former businessman who now found himself walking bald and bare-footed in an exotic city at dawn, wearing a robe and accepting food from complete strangers in total silence. And the oddest thing was, it felt *right*.

The first time I returned from binderbaht alone it took me some time to recover from the extraordinary experience. I was humbled by the kindness of the people and at the same time spiritually uplifted by this simple little ceremony that takes place hundreds of thousands of times every morning throughout Thailand. It took me a while to sort out my thoughts and emotions, but I realised that the people gave not just to the monk as an individual but to the order of monks—the

Sangha—and when they pay their respects it is to the robe and all it symbolizes for them. And the respect seemed totally genuine.

The same people do not necessarily offer food every day. They may do it once a year to 'make merit' on the anniversary of the death of a parent or loved one; on their own birthday, or for some other reason known only to themselves. The almsround I followed each morning when I lived at Wat Mahadhatu took me through a small market so I was frequently offered food by the same stall holders. One lady always placed a piece of Swiss roll and a carton of milk in my bowl, another an apple. Once I was given a cheese sandwich. I was quite touched that people were taking the trouble to offer food that they thought the Phra Farang might like, though the type of food offered or received is of little importance.

Each day I returned from binderbaht and sat cross-legged on the floor of my tiny room in Section 5 to eat breakfast in solitude and contentment. Even after a few weeks I found I was beginning to forget the businessman that I once had been and it became increasingly difficult, and unnecessary, to relate to his pleasures and desires. He was someone who once lived a very different lifestyle in a distant land and a seemingly distant past. I was beginning to find a new and hitherto unknown satisfaction in my life, a spiritual satisfaction, that I had not really experienced before. Slowly I was becoming a monk, on the *inside* as well as the outside.

Chapter 8

I haven't lived at Wat Mahadhatu for a couple of years but on the two or three occasions annually when I need to go to Bangkok I stay in Section 5, and am happy to do so. There are always many monks there as temporary residents that I do not know, but there are also a number who live there semi-permanently whilst studying at the university. With these monks I believe I have a perfectly good relationship, within the limits of our communication skills, and we are polite and helpful to each other. With the few who can speak English, I seem to have a particularly good relationship and some of them go out of their way to 'look after' me. But we didn't start off that way.

A month or so after my ordination Phra Maha Laow and Acharn Amara Thera had both returned to London and I began to feel alone and isolated in Section 5. Although I was sure some of the monks must have been able to speak English they seemed to be a most un-friendly bunch. The spirit of comradeship and brotherhood that I had expected to find in the Sangha didn't appear to include me. Some of the monks had been friendly to me before I ordained, at least to the point of smiling, but the smiles had disappeared and had been replaced by total blankness.

I was taking a shower when another Section 5 monk actually spoke to me after I had ordained. I had only been in the shower a few minutes when the monk tapped on the door and said impatiently in English: "Do you know the meaning of hurry up?". "Yes" I said. "Well, hurry up". I hurried and when I emerged from the shower the monk was waiting outside, looking quite surly. He was only a young man though as a monk obviously my senior. At a time not so long before I might have reacted, or over-reacted, aggressively to this but I was determined to be less confrontational so I quietly apologised in Thai and gave him a respectful 'wai'.

At that time I could hardly speak any Thai but I wanted to be friendly and tried speaking in both Thai and English to some of the other monks and novices. Often they would not even acknowledge what I had said or if I had tried to speak in Thai would simply laugh. On one occasion I approached a monk that I knew spoke English well, in fact it was the monk who had been impatient with me at the shower. "I understand you have been studying English for many years. You must be fluent", I said. "Yes, I am" he replied and walked away.

I started to think they were rather a snooty lot and either disliked me personally, which I could accept, or that there was some resentment against foreign monks in general. Some of the temple boys were particularly impolite and would quite openly snigger at me or behave in ways that I was sure would be unacceptable to a Thai monk, even a very new one. I didn't know the reason for any of this so I could see no way to improve the situation.

I am naturally shy but even more so with Thai people. I am constantly aware that Western and Thai cultures are very different and it is easy to be unintentionally impolite or offensive, either through actions or words. Thai society is rigidly structured; the Sangha even more so, and I had to be very cautious about my speech and behaviour. Short-time visitors to Thailand probably don't notice this as much because they usually only meet Thai people who frequently have more understanding of Western ways than the visitor has of Thai ways. To hotel staff, tour operators, restaurateurs and so on, the tourist is the customer and is therefore likely to be forgiven for any social or cultural blunder. The Thais are usually a very forgiving and easy-going people anyway.

Some aspects of behaviour which are acceptable in Western societies are most certainly not so in Thai society. For example, in the

West there is no particular taboo about touching another person on the head. In Thailand doing so is to be about as impolite as one can be.

How you move your feet is also very important. In the West we use our feet for much more than helping us stand upright or walk. We open and close doors with them, move things at floor level with them and even have household gadgets like vacuum cleaners which are designed to be operated with them. We frequently use our feet as an extra pair of hands, to the point where in Thailand Westerners' feet are often referred to as 'farang hands'. In Thailand to use the feet for almost any purpose other than walking is generally unacceptable and to point a foot at another person, especially at a monk or Buddha image and most especially at the head can cause great offence.

I was aware of these and other potential cultural pitfalls because I had taken the trouble to learn from my Thai friends in London, but I knew there must be many others of which I had no knowledge. Was I unconsciously and unintentionally breaking some cultural or religious taboo? I couldn't think of anything but I became so unhappy and concerned about the situation I started to stay in my room, not talking to anybody, in case I made it worse. In retrospect, *that* behaviour added to the problem because I'm sure the monks thought *I* was being snooty.

It was only by chance that I discovered my cultural understanding or lack of it was not really the problem at all. I passed two temple boys in the section one day and heard one sneeringly whisper to the other: "Star monk". Star monk? *Star* monk? What on earth did it mean? Over many lonely hours in my tiny room or sitting on the roof with the pigeons I thought about it, reviewing everything that I had done or that had happened to me since my ordination.

Slowly I began to see the problem and its various interlinked aspects and I realised that it could be a problem that would follow me wherever I went as a monk. In that I was right, for I have since been known not only as 'Star monk' but also as 'One-man show' and 'Phra Farang Superstar', though in quite different and friendlier circumstances.

The problem was that I am, quite simply, unusual. I don't mean in my physical appearance or personal habits; I don't think there's anything especially weird about me. Physically I am tall and thin and sometimes because of shyness I tend to stare into some middle distance without seeing anybody, without 'catching their eye', unless of course I am actually talking with them. All this can lead people to believe I am 'haughty', though I don't think I am at all. But my apparent haughtiness wasn't the crux of the problem.

When I was once at the visa department in Bangkok arranging for a visa extension I asked an official how many Western monks lived in Thailand. He told me there were probably no more than about a hundred at any one time and that most lived in fairly isolated international forest monasteries in the northeast of the country. There were only four or five Western monks living in Bangkok temples, he said. There are usually around 300,000 monks in Thailand and that figure can rise to nearer 500,000 in the rainy season when many Thai men ordain for a few months. Those numbers make the Phra Farang, the foreign monk, a rare sight indeed.

Additionally, I had been ordained by the abbot of Wat Mahadhatu, a famous, important and very high-ranking monk. He is an extremely busy administrator and does not usually have the time to ordain people himself. As far as I was aware I was the first Westerner to have had that honour, even though it was only because of my appointed Upachaya's sudden indisposition.

So, I was a rare Western monk and I had been uniquely ordained by a high-ranking Upachaya. But even that wasn't the total issue.

Laypeople frequently invite a section head and group of monks—always totalling nine—to take breakfast or lunch at a house. This may be the occasion of a wedding blessing, house blessing, or because the layperson wants to 'make merit' for a deceased loved one. At these ceremonies the monks chant relevant Pali blessings, are offered food and then after the meal are invariably given a small gift—toiletries or perhaps flowers—together with an envelope containing money. In my experience in rural areas this may be 20 or 50 Baht but in Bangkok is likely to be several hundred Baht. Once I received 1,000 Baht.

I hadn't then even begun to learn any of the Pali chanting, some of which is long and difficult. Yet I was being invited almost daily and sometimes twice a day to attend these ceremonies where I would sit in silence at the end of the line of monks while they chanted. Monks sit in order of seniority so I should always have been at the far end but often the most senior monk would move me up the line so that I could sit next to him. This would *never* happen to a new Thai monk. In fact a new Thai monk would probably have to wait many months before receiving an invitation to have breakfast or lunch at a house. Being moved up the line always caused me great embarrassment because I knew it could be considered impolite by the other monks, but I could hardly refuse. I would eat the fine food that was always offered and then be given gifts and money. Because I was a novelty.

Many of the Section 5 monks rarely had the opportunity to attend these ceremonies because they had to go to university everyday and spent most of their free time in study. Most of them, I think, worked very hard indeed, not just at their university subjects but also studying Pali chanting.

I was sure they were not so much concerned about the money I was being given. (I never kept it. It always went into the section's donation box.) However, they were understandably beginning to resent all the 'special' treatment and attention I was receiving. There were many examples of this, even within the section. One particularly embarrassing incident was when a very important Thai lady visited me at the section's reception area and presented me with a beautiful folding lecture chair which I kept, and 4,000 Baht, which I didn't. Unfortunately she was rather rude to the monks at reception and gushingly over-polite and respectful to me. That didn't endear me to the other monks at all, though why I should be held responsible for other people's good or bad manners is beyond me.

I was a brand new monk who knew nothing, but I was being treated like a celebrity. I was being photographed and videoed every time I stepped out of the monastery and was generally getting the 'star treatment'. Perhaps my apparent haughtiness added to that impression. I totally understood the resentment that seemed to be building against me because of all this and I rather resented it myself. I didn't want to be a celebrity or 'star monk' and be shown off because I had novelty value. Like my colleagues in Section 5, I wanted to study the Dhamma, meditation and the Vinaya and I wanted to become a good monk: an ordinary monk.

I couldn't do anything about being a Phra Farang nor about the circumstances of my ordination and I found myself in a difficult and delicate position. I didn't want to offend the various section heads by refusing their invitations and I didn't even know if I was allowed to. At the same time I very much wanted to live in harmony with my fellow monks in Section 5. I certainly didn't want to be the unwitting cause of any discontent.

I really had nobody to turn to for advice. I could have approached Phra Maha Suparp, the head of Section 5, especially as he was one section head who did not constantly invite me to breakfasts and lunches. His English was good and he was a kind man, but I felt the problem in part crossed cultural barriers and that he wouldn't fully understand. If he didn't *fully* understand, I feared there might be further repercussions in the section. So I said nothing to him or anybody else and the situation got slowly worse. It got to the point where if I saw one of the monks who frequently passed on invitations to me from a section head I would hide so that I wouldn't have to accept the invitation. I didn't know what to do at all and became miserably distracted from my studies and meditation and quite desperate for somebody to talk to.

Whenever Phra Maha Laow is in Thailand he stays at Section 24 of Wat Mahadhatu and I had spent many hours in that section. There was a resident monk there, Phra Maha Weera, who I guessed must have been able to speak some English because that was part of the course he was studying at the university. Although he had frequently listened with apparent interest and understanding when I talked with Phra Maha Laow, I don't recall he had ever spoken. I think at that time he had been a monk for six or seven years and he seemed a very gentle and friendly person. He was quite big and sort of soft, not fat, and he had a pleasant open face and a rarely seen but lovely smile. Someone had given him the nickname 'Giant' which he seemed to quite like.

I went to see him one day in Section 24. It turned out that, like me, his verbal reticence was due only to shyness and he could actually speak English very well. In fact he was totally fluent and had just completed translating George Bernard Shaw's 'St Joan' into Thai! I hadn't even read it in English.

We quickly became friends—he used to say 'comrades-in-arms', no doubt influenced by St Joan—and I sometimes spent hours each day talking with him in Section 24. Often we would go out together to visit other monasteries in Bangkok where he had friends and he became my advisor about many things a new monk should know.

I explained the problem at Section 5. He was sympathetic but I don't think he fully understood it from my Western view-point. He accepted that it was a problem for me but could see no way out of it that would not cause other problems. I started to spend more and more time in Section 24 with Giant and avoiding my own section as much as possible.

Giant was just about at the end of his formal studies at the university but as part of his course he had to teach Dhamma and undertake social work in a rural monastery. He had chosen a little monastery called Wat Nahoob, which was close to his own village in the northern province of Nakhon Sawan, about 240 kilometres from Bangkok. He was to leave Wat Mahadhatu permanently in a few months but before that planned to make a visit of a few days to Wat Nahoob.

Two important things happened then which were to lead to an ending of my unhappiness in Section 5. Giant invited me to join him on his short visit to Wat Nahoob, and I fell down the stairs.

Chapter 9

I was riding my motorcycle through London one night when a Cortina appeared where no Cortina should ever be — broadside on to a 1200 cc 7-hundredweight Harley-Davidson travelling at speed. The driver had tried to jump the lights and had stalled in the middle of the junction. There was nothing to be done but hit the wretched thing dead centre. The bike came to a sudden halt, embedded in the side of the car, but I didn't. I sailed through the air trailing a screamed obscenity behind me.

When I came round in hospital, I naturally enquired first about the state of my bike and then asked how I was. The bike was wrecked but I was luckier. Nothing broken, no internal injuries. Amazingly I was only bruised and slightly battered. Years later it became apparent that I had in fact weakened both my knees when I hit the road on the other side of the car. My left knee was hurt more badly than the right. This never really caused me any problems until I started to practise sitting meditation at Wat Buddhapadipa. Even then I had no great difficulty or discomfort because my meditation was not excessive and I alternated sitting with walking meditation. However, it started to exacerbate the slight damage caused by the accident years before.

One of the reasons I ordained was to devote myself to the study and practice of meditation. Foolishly, instead of building up my meditation time slowly at Wat Mahadhatu, I went straight into long periods of sitting. Additionally, all monks spend a lot of their time on their knees, during morning and evening chanting for example, or sitting cross-legged for eating. Gradually my left knee started to throb. Then it started to swell. Then it simply started giving out on me and I would fall over. I never actually fell down the stairs but I would have done if someone hadn't been quick enough to support me.

Something had to be done and a visit to a hospital close to Wat Mahadhatu was the first limping step.

The doctor could speak English and he said the cartilage in my left knee was cracking, crumbling or whatever cartilage isn't supposed to do. He said it was not a great problem and he could operate. He showed me some photographs of what the operation entailed. I'm not especially squeamish but I wasn't really into brightly-coloured, mostly red, pictures of a leg without its rightful kneecap, particularly if it was potentially my leg.

More off-putting than the operation was the recovery time. The doctor said I would probably have to stay on crutches for a couple of months. I couldn't believe this was necessary, and said so. Couldn't something be done with lasers, masers or phasers, whatever they were called? Regrettably no. Although the excellent and very expensive private hospitals in Bangkok had the latest medical technology, public hospitals did not. They do the best they can, of course, but they just don't have the funds. But the doctor assured me he had some very sharp knives. He told me that even if I didn't have the operation, the knee would not be a great problem provided I avoided putting any strain on it, which meant not doing anything that a monk has to do everyday. He even warned me against using Asian squat-style toilets!

The last thing I felt I needed at that time was to be cooped up in Section 5 on crutches for a couple of months. I didn't think I would be able to cope with the bad atmosphere my presence seemed to be causing. But if I didn't have something done about the knee I was not going to be a very effective monk, at least not in my terms.

I made a phone call to a friend in London, a nurse, and she told me it was not always necessary to have 'cut and sew' surgery for a simple cartilage problem. In some cases, she said, it could be an in-and-out of hospital in one day job. I decided to go to England and another phone call to Wat Buddhapadipa assured me that the London temple would be able to accommodate me.

Phra Maha Laow once accused me of running away from my problems. At the time that struck me as very odd, because I had always considered that I faced my problems head-on. But his comment has always stayed with me and I still frequently examine any intended action to see if it is such a case. Yes, I wanted to be away from Section 5 for a while in the hope that my 'novelty-value' would wear off and that the situation would settle down. I couldn't see any other constructive action I could take without potentially creating more disharmony. The only course seemed to be to remove the problem—me. Anyway, the fact was that something had to be done about the knee and I had every intention of returning to Thailand after it was fixed.

I had a small sum of money in a Thai bank for just such an emergency, though I hadn't expected to need it quite so quickly, and I booked a seat on a flight to London. But not immediately. I felt that if I followed the doctor's advice and didn't put any strain on my knee there was no reason to cancel the planned visit to Wat Nahoob. I invested a few Baht in a heavyweight knee support bandage and Giant and I made our plans.

The bus from Bangkok's Mor Chit terminal takes about three and a half hours to make the 240-kilometre journey, about an hour of which is spent just getting out of Bangkok's infamous traffic. Giant and I set off later than we intended, at about 9.30 am, which meant we had to buy sandwiches and fruit to eat on the bus during the monks' lunch period.

Before I ordained I had never been particularly conscious of 'breakfast time', 'lunch time' or 'dinner time'. I ate when I was hungry regardless of the time and had never liked any aspect of my life determined or regulated by the clock. Within the obvious requirements of my business life, I ate, slept and did most other things when I felt the need.

A monk cannot be so casual. Most monks eat twice a day, a minority eat only once, but all monks must finish eating by noon and then should not eat again until the following dawn. Monks who eat twice usually have their first meal immediately after going out on binderbaht at around 6.30 - 7 am and their lunch between 11 am and noon. Others frequently have a single meal at around 10 am. Because monks know they will not be able to eat after midday, they become very conscious that they must eat before, so that they will not be hungry in the evening .

I've always been skinny and have never seemed to require much food intake, so I'm not too bothered if I miss lunch and deliberately do so if I'm undertaking a long meditation. But I'd rather not. Physical hunger can be ignored, but it can also become a discomfort and distraction to one's sense of well-being. In my experience, a comfortable, healthy body, not stuffed full of food but with sufficient for its needs, leads to a comfortable mind and good physical and mental conditions for meditation. Though I still eat as little as possible, over the months and years of my life as a monk I also have come to rely on the clock rather than the rumblings of my stomach.

Giant and I ate our fruit and sandwiches whilst being driven northwards on a good motorway but through fairly uninspiring countryside, though it became more picturesque as we got further from Bangkok.

Before setting off on our journey, I had looked up the details of Nakhon Sawan province and city in an international guide book. What little information the guide gave was very dismissive of the city and at first sight it does seem rather drab and lacking in interest, certainly compared to more well-known cities in Thailand. But, as I was to eventually realise, Nakhon Sawan is much more representative of the real Thailand than some of the other places that visitors usually include on their itineraries.

All main provincial cities in Thailand share their name with the province in which they are situated. Nakhon Sawan is theoretically in the northern region of Thailand though on a map it appears to be fairly central. The city is an important crossroads but neither it nor the province have any obvious attraction to entice the average tourist to stop off whilst enroute to Chiang Mai in the far north. In fact, it is this very lack of tourist attractions that gives Nakhon Sawan its own special character. Neither the province, the city nor the people have had to compromise in any way to cater to the whims or demands of the international tourist.

Some cities in Thailand that rely heavily on tourist income have had to make many compromises, as have the inhabitants of those cities, but Nakhon Sawan has managed to remain an ordinary little provincial city. Its skyline is dominated by the roofs of temples rather than high-rise hotels and apartment blocks. Its streets are crammed with little Chinese noodle shops rather than hamburger or pizza restaurants. There are no souvenir or postcard shops, no traffic jams, nor (as far as I am aware) strip joints or sleazy night clubs.

Through the centre of the city flows the Ping river (quite literally during the rainy season) and it is in Nakhon Sawan that the Ping joins with other rivers from the north to form the mighty Chao Phraya, the River of Kings, that runs from the province, through Bangkok and to the sea. But the beauty and calm of the river is not disturbed by the irritating buzz of long-tail speed boats. The only river traffic is the little ferry that runs from one side of the river to the other.

Nakhon Sawan is an ordinary, peaceful, little city—until February, when it goes slightly crazy.

Just as Chiang Mai is the place to be for the New Year 'Songkran' festival in April, so Nakhon Sawan city is the place to be for the Chinese New Year celebrations in February. The population of the city is about 10,000 and although if asked their nationality, most would respond 'Thai', the majority of the people are in fact Chinese. Nakhon Sawan is the China Town of Thailand.

In February, the normally drab rows of 'shop houses' are spruced-up and decorated with fairy lights and bunting and many thousands of Thai and Chinese visitors pour into the city from all over Thailand for the traditional, colourful and noisy celebrations. For three days, the atmosphere is more like that of Singapore than that of a provincial Thai city. Forty-foot-long dragons and troupes of 'lion dancers' perform in all the main streets. Many of the streets are closed to traffic and the major road junctions are spanned with red-lacquered, dragon-decorated arches, giving the city something of the look of imperial China and hundreds of red Chinese lanterns supplement the normal street lighting. At night, spectacular firework displays, street parties and traditional dance performances keep the carnival atmosphere going.

I didn't know any of that when Giant and I first arrived in the city. At first sight, it seemed as ordinary and uninteresting as the guide book had led me to believe. Giant wasted no time showing me around and instead we found a beaten-up 1960s Toyota taxi for the 40-kilometre journey to Nahoob village.

I was delighted to be out of Section 5, out of Bangkok and in the green countryside. The province isn't known for spectacular scenery but it does have a sort of soft beauty about it that I found attractive and quite reminiscent of the English countryside. There were vistas that could well have been Sussex or Norfolk, except that those counties don't have banana trees and Nakhon Sawan doesn't have windmills. Although the countryside was very flat, it was broken up occasionally in the most dramatic way by granite 'mountains'. I'm not sure if they actually qualify as mountains but that's what the Thai people call them. They were really just huge piles of rock, many hundreds of metres high sometimes, which seemed to have been dropped about the countryside quite haphazardly. Some were rounded tree-covered humps while others were treeless, broken and craggy. Some of them were very beautiful indeed and the most stunning, a sort of mini-range with multiple peaks, seemed to lie at the end of the road on which we were travelling.

Nahoob village lies in the district of Banpotphisai and we were through Banphot town in a few minutes, it is so small. I renamed it 'Pisspot', much to Giant's amusement and even now we still refer to it in that way (though it is, in fact, a very nice little town). A few more kilometres down the road and the taxi turned onto a rough dirt track lined on one side with fields of tall sugar-cane and on the other side by traditional Thai farmhouses.

At the end of the two-kilometre-long track lay our destination, the village of Nahoob, and a few kilometres beyond that were the mountains of Khao Nor.

The monastery lies at one side of Nahoob so we didn't need to drive through the village to reach it. Even at that time I had seen many different types of monastery and temple buildings. Some were huge and spectacular, others were neat and pretty and some were...well, they were like Wat Nahoob. It was a typical, ordinary, rural monastery. There will be a small Uposatha Hall, an open-sided sala or meeting hall, a small crematorium, a bell tower and a collection of other buildings and kutis, some ramshackle and made of wood (with a great deal of charm to my Western eye) and others made of breeze blocks, functional and ugly. There is usually a big, open, grassy area for temple fairs and football matches, a pond, the inevitable plot of waste land where all the rubbish is dumped and a few trees, some of which are very old. There is always a 'Bo' or 'Bodhi' tree, the type of tree under which Prince Siddhattha became the Buddha. That was Wat Nahoob. It is pretty much the same picture that can be seen in thousands of villages all over Thailand. These monasteries are not built to house priceless images or relics, nor to impress tourists, nor even to glorify the Buddha. They are working monasteries, built with funds raised by the villagers themselves to serve the needs of the village and the monks who live within the community.

Each year during the Pansa or Buddhist Lent period, the monastery will be home to at least a few of the village men, who will ordain for three or four months. Some, who have left the village to work in the big cities, will also return then to devote a few months to study the teaching of the Buddha, or simply to fulfil their social obligations and 'make merit' for their parents. During the three-month-long Pansa period, monks are not allowed to travel overnight. Each night must be spent in the same monastery and monks who usually wander from temple to temple frequently return to their own village monastery for the period.

The abbot of Wat Nahoob and the one other resident monk were both away from the monastery when we arrived, so I took the opportunity to wander around on my own. The monastery covered four or five acres and in one corner was a group of old trees, shrubs and twenty-foot-tall strands of bamboo; a remnant perhaps of a forest that may well have covered much of the area years before. Inside the mini-forest was a shady clearing and I sat there on a fallen tree enjoying the smells and sounds of the forest and the clean air, so wonderfully pure after having breathed Bangkok's fumes for a couple of months.

Through a break in the trees I could see a vast expanse of paddy fields stretching away into the distance to the base of the mountains, hazy in the afternoon sun. A bright green metre-long snake slithered across the clearing; huge butterflies of the type usually seen pinned in a glass box fluttered on black and yellow wings through the trees; a chameleon clung to a branch only feet away from me, its head cocked and regarding me seemingly without fear. The silence was broken only by small sounds in the undergrowth and the occasional bird call.

I sat for more than an hour in the cool shade. My unhappiness in Section 5 came into my mind, but I let the thoughts drift away. It really didn't seem the time or place for such worries. I felt my body and mind relaxing and just enjoyed each moment with no particular identifiable thoughts to disturb me. My mind seemed to become quite calm and I slipped easily into meditation.

Giant eventually came looking for me and said that the abbot, Acharn Waow, had returned and we walked back to the main kuti block to meet him. Giant must have already told him I had a problem with my knee for as I started to kneel to offer my respects with a triple bow, he indicated that it wasn't necessary and that I should sit in whatever position I found most comfortable.

Acharn Waow could not speak English but with Giant to translate we had a long and very friendly conversation. He was in his mid-50s I think and had been a monk for more than 30 years. Nahoob was his home village and his mother and other family members still lived there. He seemed to be related to just about everybody in the village, though Thai people frequently refer to 'my brother' or 'my cousin' even when there is no blood relationship. It can be very confusing but usually doesn't matter.

The abbot was tall for a Thai, at about 6'2" the tallest I had ever met, and he was very thin. His height and build gave him a sort of stateliness which wasn't in the least bit diminished by the 18-inch-long pink plastic backscratcher he carried. This piece of 1950s Americana had a little curled hand at one end. I never saw Acharn Waow actually scratch himself with it. I'm not even sure if he knew what it was for, though he seemed to find many other uses for it. Senior monks are allowed a little eccentricity.

I began to like Acharn Waow almost immediately. Many senior monks I have met seemed to have developed a deep calmness, or 'coolness', but this has sometimes seemed to be at the expense of any trace of compassion. Or perhaps they have reached some higher level of compassion* that I do not yet comprehend. Acharn Waow seemed to be 'cool', but he also seemed to be a very caring and compassionate man, in an ordinary sense, with a deep concern for the well-being of the villagers who were under his spiritual care. To me he became Acharn Wow and for good measure with an exclamation mark — Acharn Wow!

The abbot told me I was very welcome at Wat Nahoob and that I was to relax and enjoy my visit to the countryside. One of the temple boys had prepared rooms for Giant and me in the main kuti where the abbot and another monk, Phra Maha Pern, also lived. Drinking water, bedding, an electric fan, towel, soap and toothpaste had all been laid out for me but I was sure this consideration was not at all because I was a Phra Farang or especially honoured in any way. It was a simple and polite welcoming gesture which I knew would have been extended to any visiting monk.

Wat Nahoob owned a car, another 30-year-old Toyata donated by a villager, and Acharn Waow had arranged for one of the village men to drive us to Khao Nor the following day so that I could see the mountain's monkeys.

By the time we had finished chatting it was late afternoon and I very much wanted to take a walk through the village. Giant accompanied me in case I gave the villagers too much of a shock. Most of them had never seen a farang before, let alone a Phra Farang.

Nahoob village was a collection of about 150 houses spread over a wide area and surrounded on all sides by paddy fields and sugarcane plantations. Most of the houses were built in traditional Thai style; not the Thai style seen in picture postcards, but ordinary houses for ordinary country people. All the houses were made of wood, though rarely of teak, with many gaps in the walls to allow breezes to flow through and with corrugated tin or asbestos roofs. Most stood on stilts to protect them from floods and from at least some of the local unfriendly wildlife. There were frequently concrete additions to the houses and lots of ramshackle wooden barns, rice stores and huge stone water barrels for storing rain water in case the village wells dried up.

Occasionally, I saw beautiful old buffalo carts in barns, rarely used since rural mechanisation has been so strongly promoted by successive Thai governments. The old businessman in me immediately surfaced to wonder what one would be worth to a country pub in England, parked outside in the beer garden and full of flowers. There were ducks and chickens everywhere, seemingly under no sort of control and I wondered how anybody could know which belonged to whom. Presumably the ducks and chickens know to whom they belong. Some chickens were kept for eggs and others for the much loved Thai 'sport' of cock-fighting.

On the whole, Nahoob seemed a neat and tidy village though inevitably, as in every Thai village I have ever seen, there were many unsightly piles of plastic bottles, broken glass and other household refuse. These were eyesores of course—no doubt to the villagers as well—but there is no weekly rubbish collection in rural areas, nor municipal tips where rubbish can be taken, nor the recycling bins that have become a common feature in European towns. Although Thai people are natural recyclers, especially in rural areas, some household rubbish is left to pile up, to be dispersed eventually by the wind, dogs and children.

There was nothing in the village that a Westerner would call a shop, though a few houses had open fronts and sold a small selection of everyday essential items. One had seasonal fruit, vegetables and cheap whisky, another had toiletries and cheap whisky and another had petrol and cheap whisky. Nahoobians obviously liked a drop of whisky now and again.

The one exception to the traditional and slightly decrepit houses was a very large, new concrete 'Western-style' house, with its new paint gleaming brilliantly white and contrasting starkly with the surrounding drab, wooden structures. All over Thailand, in villages and 'new towns', Thai architects have taken the general shape of the 1930s detached English suburban villa and added to it. They've added Romanesque pillars, Georgian windows, Victorian ballustrades, Art Deco doors, balconies with Greecian statuary of flowing ladies holding globular electric lamps and lots of other decorative touches that would probably give a European architect a nervous breakdown. However, the Thai people who live in them like it. The Nahoob house wasn't unattractive even though it did look out of place. I wondered if in 20 or 30 years all the old wooden houses would be gone, to be replaced by this type of house, with concrete roads and pavements instead of the dirt tracks and buffalo paths.

We met many villagers on our walk, mostly old people, for all the younger men and women were working in the paddy fields. I saw very few young children and when I mentioned this to Giant, he said they were there, but they were hiding because they were frightened of me! A lot of the old people knew Phra Maha Weera because he had been born in a village nearby and was a frequent visitor to Wat Nahoob. They all greeted him very courteously and there was obviously a great deal of respect for him in the village. I don't think they knew what to make of me at first because they had never seen anything quite like me before, but at least nobody whipped out a camera or camcorder.

A few people asked me polite questions: did I like Thai food, Thai weather, Thai people and so on, but I was amazed and delighted that even after a few minutes they just seemed to consider me an ordinary new monk and had little interest beyond the normal politeness they would extend to any visitor. They seemed to be a pragmatic people. They were easy to like, especially some of the old ladies. After a lifetime spent working in the paddy fields bending to plant seedlings, some of them couldn't straighten up anymore and were permanently bent at right-angles from the hips. But without exception they had beautiful smiles on their lined and lovely old faces, and they smiled frequently. That night I sat alone on the balcony of the kuti block listening to the night sounds and sipping at a cup of cocoa. I really felt at peace and perhaps for the first time understood the much-used Thai word 'sabbai'. It can mean healthy, well or comfortable, depending on the context, but it can also mean much more. It can be a deep inner feeling of well-being and contentment; of being at peace with oneself and with the environment. Sabbai. That's how I felt as I drifted off to sleep.

* Compassion (Karuna) is one of the four qualities of states of consciousness that Buddhism teaches should be cultivated. The others are loving-kindness or universal good-will (Metta), sympathetic joy (Mudita) and equanimity (Upekkha). These are frequently used as subjects for meditation.

Chapter 10

It's amazing how many people you can fit into an old Toyota if you really try. The Thais are wonderful at this and genuinely seem to enjoy going on a journey with someone else's elbow in their ear. And there's always room for another 'brother', 'sister' or 'cousin'. I'm not actually sure how many people were crammed into the car for the outing to Khao Nor but it was considerably more than the manufacturer's recommended number.

The drive to the mountain was quite splendid, following a meandering dirt road alongside rice paddies and sugar-cane plantations, through shady bamboo groves, remnants of forest and past delightful little streams, their surfaces covered with lotus flowers. Dotted about in the fields were enormously tall and straight teak trees, once a source of great wealth to Thailand but now, with stocks greatly diminished, it is illegal to cut them.

At the foot of the mountain lies a monastery, Wat Khao Nor, which extends a little way up the mountain itself to several cave kutis for monks who want to meditate in isolation. The monastery had an interesting collection of very realistic concrete sculptures illustrating basic Buddhist teachings. These sculptures are quite common in the grounds of rural monasteries. One showed the 'Four sights' — the four types of people Prince Siddhattha saw on secret journeys from his palace: a sick man, an old man, a corpse and an ascetic. The first three caused him to realise the suffering that all people must endure and the fourth showed him possible release from it. Another sculpture was a very realistic pile of skulls, and there was one of Prince Siddhattha as an ascetic, sitting in meditation, every vein standing out from his skeletal body but his face serene.

Apart from a striking new Uposatha Hall, the monastery was a rather scruffy, dusty place, but it's probably hard to keep anywhere clean and tidy when it's home to several hundred monkeys. Almost every hill and mountain in Thailand seems to have its share of these mischievous animals. The monkeys at Khao Nor were clever and quite capable of opening a car boot or bonnet in their endless search for edible tit-bits. They would even make a grab at a monk's bag and run off with it. The babies were cute but some of the adult males were aggressive and dangerous. Visitors to the monastery were occasionally bitten.

Giant and some of the villagers decided to climb to the top of one of the mountain's lower peaks but this actually meant *climbing*. There was a marked trail but in places it was a case of hauling oneself up fairly sheer rock faces and clinging to exposed tree roots for support. Although the doctor in Bangkok hadn't specifically mentioned avoiding mountain climbing, I'm sure he would have done if he had thought of it. I decided to go only a little way up to a flat ledge that extended over the rock face.

I sat on the ledge alone with a bottle of water looking out over miles of paddy fields. Some had been flooded after planting and others were already a brilliant green with the growing rice. The sun sparkled on the water and the intermittent squares of bright colour. Amid distant clumps of trees I could see the multi-tiered, multi-coloured roofs of several monasteries glistening in the afternoon sun. It was a view straight from a guide book to Thailand; the real Thailand, rural Thailand, a land of small villages where the vast majority of people spend their lives in back-breaking rice farming.

A few monkeys came to pester me for a while but soon lost interest and I was left alone. The only sounds were the distant and diminishing voices of Giant and the villagers as they ascended to the top of the mountain. Below me in the tree tops, monkeys dashed madly from branch to branch, seemingly rarely still and I thought for a long time about the famous Buddhist simile of 'the monkey mind'—the mind that must be trained to stop its constant movement before it can know real peace. I tried to stop even those thoughts from moving in my mind and settled into meditation. Once when I opened my eyes I found a youngish monkey had joined me on the ledge and was sitting only a few feet away, watching me intently. I wanted it to come closer, but it ran off as soon as I moved. I was reminded of an occasion years before in London when I was walking in the heavily-wooded part of Wat Buddhapadipa's grounds. I saw a young Thai monk, sitting on a log, deep in meditation, his face serene. Sitting on the palm of his hand was a squirrel, busily washing its face. Each seemed oblivious to the other. It was a beautiful scene but I crept quietly away, not wanting to disturb either of them. How much I wanted to achieve that same absolute stillness of body and mind!

After about an hour, the voices of Giant and the villagers became louder as they descended the mountain, dirty and sweaty but obviously having much enjoyed their exercise. It was a happy and peaceful afternoon and as we drove back to Nahoob I looked frequently through the car's rear window at Khao Nor. It was silhouetted against the setting sun and looked magical and mysterious, in fact I think I preferred it more from a distance than close to. I don't like monkeys much anyway.

That evening I had another long chat with Acharn Waow, the village headman and some of the people I hadn't met on my tour of the village. Everybody was very friendly and polite to me but in a perfectly straightforward and honest-seeming way.

The following morning we were to return to Bangkok and Acharn Waow had arranged for a driver to take us to Nakhon Sawan bus station in the car. As we were saying goodbye to the abbot he spoke at length with Giant. This was mostly about Giant's future duties at the monastery and I let my attention wander around the abbot's room. Photographs of famous monks lined the walls, including one of my own Upachaya; calendars, some years out of date, were pinned one on top of the other; a board showed a list of names of villagers who had donated towards building the Uposatha Hall years before............

Suddenly my attention was brought back to the conversation as I heard Acharn Waow mention my name. I didn't understand everything he said but I picked up the key words:

"...Peter...Pansa.....nii ?"   "Peter....Pansa.....Here?"

Giant never had a chance to translate. "Yes", I said immediately. And I bowed in respect and gratitude to my new abbot.

It's not really that simple of course, for a new monk has responsibilities to his Upachaya just as the Upachaya has responsibilities to those he ordains. The new monk is supposed to stay at his 'home' temple for five years, serving his Upachaya and being taught by him. I wasn't at all sure if the abbot of Wat Mahadhatu would allow me to leave that monastery and go gallavanting off to the wilds of Nakhon Sawan after only a few months. Certainly it would be unusual, but I very much wanted to go. I wondered if in this instance my unwelcome 'special' status could be made to work for me.

It would have been totally impractical for me to go to live at Wat Nahoob on my own. I could not speak Thai and Acharn Waow could not speak English so we could not communicate effectively. There was nobody in the village who could translate for us. Of course I would eventually learn Thai, I'm still telling myself that, but to be able to talk in Dhamma or Vinaya terms requires considerably more than the sort of 'tourist Thai' which can be picked up relatively easily.

I also needed a lot of help to learn some of the Pali chanting. Chanting has never been particularly important to me personally but it is of great importance to many Thai people. There are some passages which are used frequently and which every monk should know. Besides spending time in his meditation and Dhamma study, almost every monk has contact with the laypeople at some time, especially at 'cycle of life' ceremonies. At funerals, for example, monks chant passages concerned with the impermanence of all things and these passages are a great comfort to those who have been bereaved. It would have been immensely difficult for me to learn the chanting without guidance.

But I wasn't going to be on my own. Giant would be there and he was both willing and able to be my teacher. Apart from his fluency in English, he was also a 'Maha', a title earned by a monk following an examination to test his proficiency in Pali, so he was very capable of teaching me to chant correctly. He would also, we thought then, be able to teach me Thai, though as it turned out that was a rather optimistic idea.

We sat in Section 24 for many hours discussing — plotting — how we could convince the abbot to allow me to go to Nakhon Sawan. At the same time I had to tell him I needed to return to England, though I didn't think that would be such a problem because it was a medical necessity and I would be back before the Pansa started. We made an appointment to see the abbot and, as usual, I was very nervous when we went to his section with our request .

Phra Sumethadhibodi is a very busy man with far-reaching responsibilities. I have only ever seen him surrounded by monks and laypeople, with a queue waiting for advice, or to have a form or letter signed, or on some other religious business. Every time I have seen him he has been sitting on the floor of his room surrounded by two-foot-high untidy piles of paperwork, files, photographs and books, but despite the apparent lack of organisation he is known to be a very organised man indeed.

He has a wonderful air of controlled calmness about him. After someone has spoken to him, he frequently remains quite still for a moment before replying. If a question has been asked, there is no expression on his face, no 'body language', to give a hint as to what his answer is going to be.

Our turn in the queue came and we made our most respectful bows to him. My robe fell off. Giant did all the talking and he talked for a long time. I constantly searched the abbot's face for some indication as to how he felt about what was being said, but apart from the occasional glance at me, when I quickly lowered my eyes, there was no reaction at all. No hint of approval or disapproval.

Giant stopped talking. There was a silence. "Yes", said the abbot. It was settled. I could go. We bowed again and much to everybody's surprise my robe stayed on.

I was going to England. I was going to get my knee sorted out. And then I was going to live at Wat Nahoob.

Chapter 11

Anybody unfamiliar with Wimbledon could probably drive down Calonne Road and be completely oblivious to the fact that hidden behind one of its grander houses is one of the most extraordinary buildings in Europe. It can hardly be seen from the road at all, except in winter when the screening trees have lost their leaves, then the sun glinting off the orange-glazed roof tiles might attract the eye. Drivers sometimes come to a screeching halt and reverse their cars back down the road for confirmation that what they thought they saw was not an exotic illusion.

On a man-made rise, behind a large turn-of-the-century mansion, set in four acres of gardens and woodland, stands a Thai temple. A real Thai temple. This is not a building that compromises in any way to Western architectural taste. It is straight from Thailand and, from the outside at least, could be seen replicated all over that country.

It is small but it rises from its marble base with proportions that make it appear larger and grander than it is. It positively glows as the sun reflects off the gold leaf and mosaics of coloured glass that decorate its pillars, roofs and doors. Little bronze bells with Bodhi leaf shaped pendants tinkle in the eaves, and on the roof massive golden hook-like finials called 'jo fa' rear into the sky.* This is the Uposatha Hall of Wat Buddhapadipa.

Inside it is even more extraordinary and there is nothing like it even in Thailand, or anywhere else for that matter. Its walls, every square inch of them, are covered with mural paintings. Not the traditional murals of Thai temples, for here within the story of the Buddha's life are characters well-known to Westerners; Charlie Chaplin, Superman, Presidents Nixon, Reagan and Bush, Colonel Qaddafi, Saddam Hussein, Ninja Turtles and many more. Elephants stand side by side with nuclear missiles; airplanes and spacecraft fly across painted skies with 'heavenly beings'; a Henry Moore sculpture and Stonehenge occupy the same wall panel and isn't that Margaret Thatcher over in one corner directing things? Like it or not, it is a most incredible artistic achievement and took 14 artists seven years to complete, sometimes working with the tiniest of brushes under magnifying glasses for the most detailed work.

Before I ordained, I sat in this building for many hours, examining every panel, and even then I did not see it all. For there are hidden things too, known only to the artists and they have long since returned to Thailand, their great effort rewarded with not a single coin. It was their way of 'making merit' and contributing to the spread of Buddhism in the West.

The Uposatha Hall houses the temple's main Buddha image, a massive 700-year-old bronze work from the Sukhothai period of Thai history. Originally perhaps the image may have been covered in gold, but now it gleams dully black, reflecting the gold of a second large image from a later period. On each side stands an almost life-sized image of the leading disciples of the Buddha—Sariputta and Moggallana. There is also a reproduction of the Emerald Buddha, though it conveys little of the beauty of the original in Bangkok's Wat Phra Kaew.

Wat Buddhapadipa was originally located in a small house in East Sheen in 1965 at the invitation of British Buddhists. It was the first Thai monastery to be established outside of Thailand. The present much larger premises were acquired in 1976 so that the Uposatha Hall could be built but also because of the increasing interest in Buddhism throughout Europe, with a corresponding increase of visitors and students to the monastery.

There are usually nine Thai monks in residence. They live in the main house and some of them have been resident in England for many years.

Wat Buddhapadipa is very much a working monastery. The monks are missionaries and they have a job to do which they undertake with great enthusiasm and energy. Besides teaching meditation for beginners and advanced students at weekly classes, there are also week-long residential retreats. There are classes in basic Buddhism and in the Abhidhamma, or Buddhist metaphysics, and the monks are frequently invited to lecture in schools and colleges all over London. They produce several monthly magazines and additionally officiate at 'cycle of life' ceremonies, mostly for the Thai community in England, at which they chant relevant Pali suttas and blessings. It is a very busy monastery but is well-supported by a large number of Thais and Europeans who visit not just for the religious environment but also to meet with others for social and cultural activities.

Soon after I started studying at Wat Buddhapadipa, I suggested to the abbot that the monastery should have a resident European monk. Although the monks speak good or excellent English there are some Pali concepts used in teaching Buddhism and meditation that are taken almost for granted in traditionally Buddhist countries but which may not always be entirely clear to the Westerner, regardless of the teacher's fluency in English. I never thought at the time that the resident European monk might one day be me.

Of course I wasn't really a resident, merely a visitor, but nevertheless in some ways I felt I had come home. Not because I was in England but more because I was at Wat Buddhapadipa. It was in this same old house, set in these same tranquil grounds, that I had realised years before that I wanted more than anything else to become a monk and to follow the teaching of the Buddha. It was here, in the meditation chamber beneath the Uposatha Hall, that I had my first lesson in walking meditation, when my dear old teacher forgot to tell his naive students to keep their eyes open, with the consequence that we ended up walking into pillars and falling over each other. Here, in these grounds on a warm summer's evening, I made my first attempt at an all-night meditation, sitting under the trees by the side of the lake and fell asleep after about 10 minutes.

It was at Wat Buddhapadipa that I first met the extraordinary men who in some cases had already spent more than 30 or 40 years in the robes and who stimulated me into asking questions on subjects which I had never even thought of before. Often they taught without knowing it, for merely by observing them, I could see the results of those years in the robes. It could be seen in their controlled movements, their calm faces, their innocent smiles and in their precise and measured reactions to any situation. And it could also be *felt*, for being with the monks was to experience that tranquillity for oneself and to share a little of what they had learned.

It was delightful for me to be back in that environment and I was happy to be able to work for the monastery and also to take part in some of the ceremonies with which the monks must be involved, despite my lack of chanting skills. I think many of the regular European visitors were also pleased to have an English monk at the monastery, even though he was a brand new one and knew little or nothing. On Sundays particularly, when many people came to study or visit, I was kept busy simply talking, though I frequently felt awkward when it became clear that many of the students knew far more about Buddhism than I.

I think my meditation teacher, Acharn Amara Thera, also saw the value of having a European monk at the temple for he asked me if I would like to stay for the Pansa in London. I was tempted, but I said 'No'. If I stayed at Wat Buddhapadipa I would naturally have to do my share of teaching, either Dhamma or meditation, and I did not feel anywhere near ready at that time. I certainly couldn't teach Dhamma but I could teach meditation, though I would be teaching others' theories and experiences from books. I wanted to teach from *my* experience. I wanted to teach what I had personally realised from my own practice. I wanted to be able to say: "This *works*. I know it works". So far I had done very little 'practising'. I explained to Acharn Amara Thera that I wanted to undertake Buddhist Lent at a remote temple where I would have little contact with people or the distractions they can cause. I wished to be where I would be able to meditate undisturbed and in isolation.

The first thing, anyway, the reason that had brought me back to England, was to get my knee fixed. If I didn't get that done I wouldn't be meditating much anywhere. A visit to a doctor was the priority item on my London agenda.

All the monks at Wat Buddhapadipa are registered with a medical practice in Wimbledon and I went to see the doctor there. He said he would arrange for an appointment with a National Health Service, NHS for short, consultant, which might take two or three months, and then if I required an operation, the hospital would make a further appointment which could well be in another three or four months. Five months or more! But the start of the Buddhist Lent was only three months away and if I didn't make it back to Thailand before then, I would have to stay in London until the end of the Pansa in October. There had to be another option. There was, but could I afford it?

Wimbledon Parkside Hospital is, as its name implies, alongside Wimbledon Common and only a short distance from the monastery. It looks like an elegant, discreet, exclusive and very expensive hotel and as soon as I walked into the reception area I added another zero to my mental estimate of what the private treatment there might cost. I would have walked straight out again if I hadn't already made an appointment.

I was shown immediately into the consulting room of the doctor who specialised in joint problems. I very much regret that I cannot remember his name for he was without doubt the kindest doctor who has ever laid hands on me. He wasn't actually titled 'doctor' anymore for he was a consultant at an NHS hospital and for some reason I have never been able to fathom had, in the way of consultants, reverted to 'Mister'.

Mr Doctor didn't seem in the least bit surprised to have a bald and orange-robed patient and didn't even make the mistake of asking me to take my trousers off. He prodded and probed at my knee and confirmed that there was a small piece of cartilage which had broken away and should be removed. I told him I had to return to Thailand quite soon and needed the operation done quickly. "How about tomorrow?" he asked. "How much will it cost?" I countered, feeling as if I was haggling in a Thai market. "£1,600 plus £75 for this consultation" he replied, with a perfectly straight face.

I'm sure his patients don't usually turn a hair at such breathtaking figures and simply reach for their gold cards. I sat calmly, trying to think of some polite way of extricating myself from the situation. We looked at each other, our faces equally expressionless, then both of us burst out laughing. "You're a Buddhist monk" he said. He was quick all right. "Why did you become a monk?" He seemed genuinely interested and we chatted for about another £50-worth of consulting time. I had to tell him that I couldn't afford the operation though I was of course, quite prepared to pay for the consultation. He told me not to worry about the £75, he wasn't going to charge me, and added that if I telephoned his secretary at the NHS hospital she would book me in for an operation on the NHS as soon as possible. He wouldn't let me jump the queue, he said, but he would slip me in between other scheduled patients and would just work a bit faster that day.

I was well used to sometimes extraordinary acts of kindness and generosity from Thai people but I was especially delighted to find it extended to me as a Buddhist monk in England. Of course, kindness and generosity should not be restricted within denominational limits and they remain the same virtuous acts whether they come from a Buddhist heart, Muslim heart or Christian heart and to whoever they are extended, but I was still greatly touched by the doctor's 'jai dee'.

A week later I checked into the NHS hospital early in the morning and was back at Wat Buddhapadipa in the afternoon. I stayed on crutches for only about a week. My knee was fixed. I could go to Nahoob.

* The 'jo fa' are always attached to an Uposatha Hall when everything else is completed. I have heard them described as 'sky hooks', their purpose being to hook the building onto heaven — alternatively I have heard that their purpose is to prevent flying demons landing on the roof.

Chapter 12

Because my problem knee was sorted out so quickly, I had ample time ahead of me to return to Thailand and take up residence at Wat Nahoob before the Pansa started in the middle of July. I decided I would stay another month or so in London to help at Wat Buddhapadipa and also take the opportunity to see some of my old friends.

During my travels to visit various people I had to make use of public transport and this sometimes led to potentially confrontational and humiliating situations, especially when waiting at a bus stop or walking to the station. The Thai monks are well-known in Wimbledon and I think they are mostly greeted politely by residents and shop-keepers, or at worst simply ignored. I believe there is occasionally some minor unpleasantness, mostly verbal insults, though on one occasion a monk had a tomato thrown at him. The monks do not respond to any of this and I am sure that as well as remaining both outwardly and inwardly calm they are also genuinely understanding and forgiving.

If anything it was worse for me. Because they look 'exotic', the Thai monks can get away with their unconventional dress and appearance to an extent. I, however, am very pale, tall, skinny and very English-looking and I often became the target for all sorts of abuse. Some people seemed to take it as a personal affront that I was not Christian. When walking in the street I was frequently followed by jeering gangs of youths or children chanting 'Hare Krishna, Hare Krishna' and so on, but that didn't really bother me too much. On one occasion, some-one threw a stone at me and on another a group of youths flicked ink down the back of my robe. It's still there, even after many hundreds of washes. Frequently people would quite openly giggle and point at me and although that was totally harmless, it occasionally made me feel like some sort of freak.

This was all the complete opposite of my reception when walking on any Thai street, but I always bore in mind my experience at Wat Phra Kaew with Phra Maha Laow a few days after I ordained. Whether people are being respectful or jeering it's much the same thing and no ego-response, no movement of the mind, is necessary. That's the theory anyway, but the practice can be considerably more difficult and I never really felt comfortable outside of the monastery.

The closest I came to physical abuse was on the underground. I foolishly got into a carriage that was occupied only by a group of teenagers and I should have known I was asking for trouble. The abuse started the moment the doors closed behind me. The boys obviously saw me as an easy target and were constantly egged-on by the girls, but at first it was just the usual bad language and idiotic insults. I kept my face as calm and as expressionless as possible, my eyes fixed on the floor in front of me, for I knew that if I responded in any way I would probably worsen the situation. In fact, my apparent calm seemed to make the boys quite angry and I realised that I was probably in for a 'bashing', especially when the boys started to leave their seats and approach me.

Though calm on the outside, my heart was pounding and I was quite scared. I thought I would get off at the next station, but then I decided against it. I would stand my ground, in a way I had to do so, and refuse to be intimidated just because I had no hair or because I was wearing a robe instead of jeans. I would remain as calm and collected as I could be and I mentally prepared myself for what was to come.

The train pulled into a station and by some miracle two uniformed policemen got into the carriage and sat on the same bench as me. I don't know if they were aware of the situation when they got in but they smiled at me and I smiled back, though I wanted to give them both a hug. The youths shut up and I continued my journey in peace.

I remembered a funny story another English monk told me. He had been visiting his home in England, in the North, I think, and he was attacked by a street newspaper seller. The man grabbed hold of the monk's alms bowl and started to beat him about the head with it, whilst screaming that he should "Come to Jesus"!

I've always believed that everything that happens, positive or negative, can be taken as a lesson and I learnt something from my experiences of walking and travelling around London. I don't think I have ever been racist or bigoted against any 'minority' group on the grounds of skin colour, religious beliefs or sexual orientation, but I began to understand and experience for myself how members of such groups probably feel when they are subjected to mindless abuse, frequently a lot worse than the mostly harmless stuff I had to put up with. I began to understand a little of their humiliation, their anger and frustration. Suddenly, in the city of my birth, *I* was a minority, *I* was the 'Paki', the 'nigger', the 'queer' and the target for anybody with a grudge against the world in general. It is an unhappy feeling. I never told any of the other monks or my friends about these and other incidents. They were something I had to face and come to terms with on my own.

I have always considered myself lucky to have made a few, just a few, very good friends in my life. I don't mean acquaintances, I mean people whom I would do virtually anything for and who I believe would do anything for me. Friends who have been friends in some cases for 10, 20, 30 years or more. I have never made friends easily but those I have made I have kept for a long time because I have worked at it, just as they have. We have sometimes drifted a little apart whilst following different interests but we have always come back together again at some point on the road, but then our 'roads' were all going in roughly the same direction.

My friends had seen me at my lowest moments and they had been supportive. They had seen me during my 'highs' and they had rejoiced in my happiness or good fortune. We had stuck together in relationships that seemed indestructible by time, distance or circumstance.

The last time I had seen any of my friends in England I had been a layman. I was then living under the eight precepts of an Upasaka and had some restrictions on my behaviour, but nothing that really affected our relationships very much. Now I was a fully-fledged monk living under the 227 rules of the Vinaya and I wondered what my friends' reactions would be and whether our relationships would change drastically.

Naturally I didn't expect them to greet me in the same way that a Thai person greets a monk—with a graceful 'wai' and sometimes a triple bow and always deferentially referring to the monk as 'Luang Pi' or 'Luang Por'— 'Respected Brother' or 'Respected Father'. Some of my friends had known me for a very long time and had seen me in situations and circumstances that were not at all 'respectable'! They would not be treating me as though I had suddenly turned into a 'holy man', that was for sure.

In the event, reactions to my changed physical appearance ranged from screams of delighted mock horror to embarrassed laughter. Some of my friends reacted as though I'd just popped out for a minute: "Oh, hello Pete, come in...." that sort of thing, and put the kettle on for a cup of tea, just like old times. My only aunt, a lovely 75-year-old, completely ignored my appearance and flung her arms around me and gave me a big kiss, totally against the monks' rules but I wasn't going to spoil an old lady's pleasure by telling her she couldn't hug me anymore. One friend of more than 30 years standing met me at his local railway station with a paper bag over his head so he would be spared the embarrassment of being seen with me! This was very amusing of course, as it was meant to be, but there was a more serious side to some of these reunions.

The rules that monks live by are to be practised in every waking moment, not just when the monk is 'on duty' at a religious ceremony or in the public eye. Even when he is entirely alone, the monk should not relax his vigilance, his 'mindfulness' of his behaviour. He should develop his behaviour until he is relaxed according to the rules of the

Vinaya; until following the rules becomes natural and comfortable for him. He cannot live his life by one set of rules in public and another in private.

I remember reading something a monk wrote which has always stayed with me: "When you are with a lot of people, behave as though you are alone. When you are alone, behave as though you are with a lot of people". In other words, keep to one standard, the standard set by the Vinaya.

I do change some aspects of my behaviour when I move from Thai culture to English culture, but that is really just exchanging one set of social norms for another. As long as I don't have to compromise my position as a Buddhist monk, nor go against the spirit of the Vinaya, my mind is untroubled.

With one exception, my friends are not Buddhists and know nothing about Buddhist meditation, the Dhamma or the Vinaya. There is no reason why they should. When I arrived on various doorsteps, they saw an old friend who was now dressed in robes instead of jeans and a tee-shirt, or the business suit that they were more accustomed to. That was probably not too hard for them to accept, but I don't think any of them could fully accept or understand that through my practice I was actively seeking and encouraging change and development to occur within *myself*; to develop the very thing that they had loved just as it was before — me, Peter Robinson. They could see the robe wrapped around my body but they couldn't see it was also wrapped around my heart.

All my friends were interested in my new life and tried hard to understand why I couldn't do this, or had to do that, as a monk. But without an understanding of what the Buddha taught, why he taught it, and a knowledge of the background of the Vinaya rules, their understanding had to be superficial. There was sometimes an awkwardness between us that we were all aware of and which had never existed before. I felt especially embarrassed about this because I knew it was the changes in me, rather than any changes in them, which were the cause.

One friend of more than 20 years standing, seeking to be honest, wrote to me: "Understand if some of us might be human enough to be embarrassed, after so many years, by having to call you by your chosen name or to go out with you in your robes. You have changed, we have not".

I cannot quantify the changes which are happening within me. I know that my practice of meditation and my life style are helping to develop certain qualities, and to rid me of others, but any change is such a gradual process that I cannot see it, nor do I have any way of measuring it. Each day I am what I am, and if I am even a tiny bit 'better' today that I was yesterday then I have made progress. Just putting on the robe does not itself bring about any great change. It is the practice of meditation and of living the Dhamma and Vinaya that achieves the goal.

What my friends called my 'monkish behaviour' was already mostly quite natural to me, but it will never be natural to them. I know most of my friends have great respect for what I am doing, even if they don't fully understand the 'why' or 'what for'. They try hard to adjust to my new circumstances but it must be extremely difficult for them. Understandably, they want me to be the same old Peter that they have known for so long. But it cannot be.

It is fundamental to the Buddha's teaching that all things are impermanent and subject to change and eventual decay. Perhaps some of my old friends and I will eventually drift irrevocably apart because our lives are now so different. I can identify with their lives because I've done it all and shared the same aspirations and dreams. But they will never be able to identify with mine, no matter how much they want to or how much they try. This was a great sadness for me.

The warm weather was approaching in England and the rain clouds were gathering in Thailand. It was time to leave. On my last evening at Wimbledon, I sat in the monastery's meditation garden in a little clearing on the edge of the lake. The lights of the Uposatha Hall were on and the building was brilliantly reflected in the still water. I sat there for a long time, as I had done on so many occasions in the past, relishing the beauty and silence of the evening and letting my thoughts wander where they liked. They frequently wandered to another clearing, another monastery, 10,000 kilometres away, to the place that was not only to be my new home but also my meditation 'workshop'.

I felt ready. Most of the practicalities of the monks' daily life were familiar to me. Now it was time to start the real work. I knew it wasn't going to be easy. I didn't know it would be quite so hard.

Chapter 13

I was to live at Wat Nahoob for more than a year. My days usually passed pleasantly, peacefully and productively. Most days were much the same, as I knew they would be, as I needed and wanted them to be, and I slowly began to develop a very strong feeling of being at peace with myself: Sabbai. An observer, especially a Western observer, would probably have considered my life to be boring, but that depends on one's point-of-view, or perhaps on one's personal definition of the word. My life wasn't boring to me, for although the days followed much the same routine and I had few duties, I was conscious of continuous small changes in me that I would possibly not have been able to recognise, acknowledge or even experience at Wat Mahadhatu, Wat Buddhapadipa or anywhere else.

These changes were not obvious on a day-to-day basis, but I would occasionally find myself thinking something, doing something or reacting to something in quite a different way and with a different attitude to how I might once have reacted. I also found sometimes that I genuinely seemed to have no reactions or attitudes at all, neither negative nor positive. My whole perspective on life seemed to be gradually changing. Slowly—very slowly—I felt I was becoming more of an observer; an observer of what was happening around me as well as what was happening to me and within me.

Because even in small ways I could actually see and experience for myself that the Buddha's teaching worked, each day brought a strengthening of purpose and a new commitment to my life as a monk. There was to be a black, confused period when I was full of despair, feeling lost, alone, and believing that I lacked not only the strength to continue but also any sense of where I was going, but with the Dhamma as my support, I persevered.

Although the environment at Wat Nahoob was the right one and helpful for me at that time, I was conscious of the danger of becoming too attached to it, or allowing myself to think that any 'results' from my practice were due to the environment. They weren't. The peaceful and untroubled environment was merely an aid to help me, just as the robes were an aid and just as the cushion I used for sitting meditation was an aid. Any progress or lack of it in my meditation was not due to the cushion; its job was to make me less aware of the hard floor and allow me to settle into meditation quickly, easily and comfortably. The results of my meditation and every other aspect of my life was concerned only with my 'state of mind'.

I believe my sense of well-being and any progress I thought I was making in my meditation was due as much to what I didn't have as to what I had. At Wat Nahoob, I had everything I needed for my physical and spiritual nourishment, and nothing more. I had a pleasant environment, a pleasant companion if I needed company, a roof over my head and sufficient food. I had my books and my purpose. What I didn't have was pressure: pressure to be, to do, to achieve anything. I wasn't even under any self-imposed pressure to achieve 'results' in my meditation. I had a meditation programme but it didn't have a timetable. As far as I was concerned, I was just doing it and was content to see what, if anything, I would learn.

I also didn't have much in a material sense to 'cling' to or become 'attached' to, which I was beginning to realise quite clearly for myself had been the very cause of much of my unacknowledged or subconscious previous discontent. Through my meditation, I began to see just how much clinging I had done in the past—clinging to things, to people, to ideas and concepts. I saw how all this clinging and attachment had led to what had been a largely unsatisfactory life. It had been fun on the surface, but trivial and not satisfying in any deep sense,

it had lacked real purpose. It was only when I slowly began to recognise these conditions and worked towards eradicating them that I saw
just how much clinging I had been doing. I began to see also that all
my previous ambitions and desires, my seeking after material
success, comfort and sensual diversions, and my blind acceptance of
society's values had been largely pointless. I had been side-tracked
and deluded.

Some months after I moved to Wat Nahoob, I wrote to a friend in
England: "It is difficult for me to explain what a joy my life has become. Every 'now' in my life is just right; just as it should be, just as
it is, and even the occasional not-so-good moment is just a fleeting
occurrence that affects me only if I let it. The 'now' quickly becomes
the 'then' and is forgotten. But there are few not-so-good moments
anymore. Wat Nahoob, here, now, is the place I am and the place I am
content to be. There is nothing I miss, nothing I want. There's no
'I wish....' or 'If only....' "

I worked hard at my meditation and for a time I was profoundly
content. I don't think there had ever been a period in my life when I
had felt so genuinely and deeply content, though I think few of my
friends in England really understood why. In my letters to them, I
would usually only write about the practicalities and routine of my
life rather than any deeper significance of it. I didn't want to seem to
be 'lecturing' about the spiritual satisfaction I was finding in Buddhism in case it might have appeared that I was making comparisons
with their lives. I would never do that, for I believe totally that everybody must find their own path through life. Someone else's path could
be quite different from mine, but no less satisfying to them. Being a
monk was just my way of life: it suited me but it didn't suit my friends
and that was fine.

Once when I wrote to a friend describing my daily routine he
wrote back simply 'You must be mad'. A few years before I might
well have agreed with him, but then 3.45 am was often the time I went
to bed. Now it was the time I got up. Adjusting my waking and sleep-

ing times proved quite difficult at first. I don't have any particular problem about getting up but I have never found it easy to go to sleep early. For many years I had rarely gone to bed before 1 am or 2 am, but now to get sufficient sleep, I reckoned five or six hours, I was having to go to bed at 9.30 pm. My body clock eventually adjusted, it had to, but it took rather longer than I expected and there were many mornings when I dragged myself up after only a couple of hours sleep.

I had only a few light duties at the monastery and my daily routine was simple: up at 3.45 am to ring the bell for morning chanting, out on binderbaht at about 6 am, breakfast at 7 am, lunch at 11 am and ring the bell for evening chanting at 5 pm. Periods in between were spent helping to keep the monastery grounds swept and tidy, in meditation and in study. I also gave myself the job of cleaning the Uposatha Hall and its many Buddha images each week.

Because I had the job of ringing the bell in the morning I was always the first one up. The bell was also the villagers' alarm clock, for everybody in rural Thailand tries to get as much work as possible done in the early morning before it gets too hot.

When Acharn Waow had given me the bell-ringing duty my heart had sunk and I was tempted to ask for another duty instead, but I didn't. The three-foot brass bell was hung at the top of a 40-foot-tall concrete tower, much like the firemen's training towers in England but with lots of red and yellow curly decoration. It wasn't the duty that bothered me, nor the height of the tower, it was the getting up there that worried me.

The tower had narrow concrete steps up to the first level but to get to the bell I then had to climb a twelve-foot-tall ladder. I do not like ladders at the best of times, no matter how sturdy their construction or how securely fixed they are. Put me halfway up a ladder and I freeze, unable to go up or down.

The ladder at Wat Nahoob was neither well-constructed nor securely fixed, in fact I don't think it really qualified as a 'ladder' at all. It was just lots of bits of rough old wood partially held together with nails and lengths of string. The so-called rungs were especially disconcerting. They were not an equal distance apart. Some were twelve inches apart and some were 16 and the ten rungs were not rounded but square, with rough splintery edges that were really painful on bare feet. This terrifying contraption went up almost vertically and disappeared through a hole in the ceiling. The most hazardous thing was that it extended only about two inches above the hole in the second floor and there was nothing to stop it slipping at the bottom.

On the first morning of my duty, I climbed about three-quarters of the way up and froze. I found myself clinging on for dear life, quite unable to move. I tried to calm myself with some deep breathing but all the time I was seeing a middle-aged Englishman, a former businessman, wearing only a sabong up a dangerous ladder in a remote Asian village at four in the morning. And I asked myself: "Why? What am I *doing*?" and other great philosophical questions to that effect. I had to give myself a good talking to before I could throw myself up the last few feet. But I made it, stood up—and cracked my bald head against the edge of the bell, almost causing me to fall back down the hole in the floor. A totally out-of-sequence 'bong' echoed across the countryside, followed by several unseemly oaths which happily were most unlikely to have been understood by any citizens of Nahoob who were already awake.

The mallet used to beat the bell had its own built-in hazards. It weighed several pounds but the head sometimes came off as it was swung and would go whizzing over the parapet, necessitating another hazardous journey on the ladder to retrieve it. There was a long sequence of about 40 strikes in the morning and for some 'notes' the bell had to be struck really hard on its rim. If I missed, the weight of the mallet plus the momentum of the swing could easily have sent me over the edge. The vibrations when the mallet came into contact with the metal would jiggle my eyeballs and nobody warned me it was necessary to steady the bell with one hand. After about a dozen strikes, the bell would be swinging about all over the place while I ducked and dived to keep out of its way, while still wildly swinging the mallet to keep the sequence going.

For several days I dreaded my early morning duty, but I found my fear of the ladder slowly disappeared until after about a week I was up and down it like a little Khao Nor monkey. I have never lost my dislike of ladders in general but that particular one became a part of my life and ceased to bother me. And I really enjoyed bell-ringing. There was great satisfaction in getting exactly the right note out of that great old bell and when I had finished I would look out over the village and watch the lights come on in the houses as a new day began for Nahoob.

For the monks the day began at 4.15 am when we would all assemble in the Uposatha Hall. Although 4.15 didn't really seem to me to be a civilised time to do anything, I always looked forward to morning chanting. It was an illogical feeling but I felt that through the chanting I was able to reaffirm my personal beliefs in my teacher and all that he taught. The Bote's main Buddha image, made from bronze and slightly bigger than life-size, was one of the most beautiful I had seen, and even though I knew intellectually it had no ultimate significance, I actually enjoyed bowing before it and what it represented.

I know many Westerners do not understand the frequent bowing monks have to do, either to images or to more senior monks, but if done mindfully and in awareness of *what* one is paying respect to, it can be a form of meditation, as can everything in the monks' life. The acoustics in the little Bote were wonderful, though I don't think my voice added anything to the harmonies. However, I always chanted with great enthusiasm and Acharn Waow never complained.

After about 30 minutes of chanting, I would usually go off to the forest for about an hour's meditation before going out on binderbaht. That was one of my favourite meditation times for the temperature was usually still cool and the local insects seemed to get up late.

At Wat Nahoob, a huge ancient drum was sounded to warn the monks and villagers that it was time to go out on binderbaht: the time traditionally being when it is light enough to see the lines on the palms of one's hands. The drum beat reverberated across the village and the surrounding countryside and was frequently faintly echoed by other drums, far away in other monasteries.

Going out on binderbaht in a rural village is quite different from in a city or town. At Nahoob we walked together in single file, followed by a rickety, old trolley pushed by a couple of rickety, old men. The villagers would be waiting outside their houses and put only steaming rice into our alms bowls. The curries, fruits and sweets would be put into little pans on the trolley. The round was quite long and took about an hour but it was always a good opportunity for reflection on the life I was leading.

I made a rather embarrassing mistake one morning whilst on binderbaht. The monk who walked directly in front of me obviously had some sort of digestive problem and was unfortunately very flatulent in the early morning. His constant 'body noises' seemed to thoroughly amuse the other monks, but they weren't immediately behind him. I decided one morning to walk at the end of the line of monks instead. As we walked through the village I became increasingly mystified by the number of knowing smiles and 'nudge nudge wink wink' type of looks I was getting from the people. Giant hadn't walked on binderbaht that morning and when we arrived back at the monastery I asked him why the villagers had seemed so amused. He roared wth laughter and explained. Apparently, being made to walk at the back of the line is frequently a punishment for a monk who has confessed to masturbating! Next day I resumed my normal place.

Some of the people who lived along the dirt track that led from the main road to the village came to see Acharn Waow one day. They were between the binderbaht routes of two monasteries, Wat Nahoob and another monastery on the main road, but monks from neither walked on binderbaht past their homes. They wanted the opportunity to 'make merit' by offering food to the monks and asked Acharn Waow if some of the monks would go out on binderbaht along the track.

Next morning Giant and I went that way instead of through the village. The track was about two kilometres long and was made from a reddish earth on which were scattered very sharp pieces of granite and other stones. It was absolute hell to walk on with bare feet and Giant and I were both limping by the time we got back to the monastery. But the abbot decided that one monk would go out on binderbaht down the track each day and I volunteered.

I'm not a masochist and I certainly didn't enjoy having my feet lacerated by the granite chips, but it was worth putting up with in return for the solitude that the track provided. Binderbaht in the village was a much more casual affair than I had been used to in Bangkok. In the village the monks were well-known to the people and all were related in some way so going out on binderbaht often turned into a sort of social outing and an opportunity to chat with family or friends. This was obviously quite natural but to me it seemed that the action of going on binderbaht had become secondary to the pleasant stroll and opportunity to socialise. I wanted to go out on binderbaht alone.

The abbot gave me a temple boy to carry the curries and other food offered, though frequently I would do without the boy and carry my own pans as well as my bowl. Because the track was so rough and used by so many vehicles, including buffalo carts, the surface had become very rutted and pot-holed. Often in the mornings these holes would be full of dirty but cool water and I took every opportunity to stop for a moment to bathe my aching feet. This seemed to amaze my temple boy but for me it was a great relief, until the boy pantomimed in very graphic detail that the puddles were actually a great relief to the buffaloes and I had been pickling my feet in their urine! I carried on doing it anyway.

Despite the difficulties of walking on the track, it was well worth it for the beauty of the surroundings at that time of the morning, not that I could enjoy it too much because I had to be mindful of every step I took. Most of the farms were set back on one side of the track and screened by trees or stands of bamboo. On the other side were miles of sugar-cane plantations. Frequently in the early morning, there would be a ground mist across the fields lying at a perfectly equal depth of several feet all the way to Khao Nor, which looked like a primeval black island rising dramatically from a white sea. Early in the morning, the air was still cool and there was never a sound from anywhere. In that peaceful, rural setting one morning, much to my surprise, the silence was broken by the most bizarre music coming from a very long way off and rolling towards me across the mist-covered fields. It was Frank Ifield yodelling!

On the whole, Nahoob was not a poor community as most of the farmers owned their land and some had fairly substantial holdings. They weren't materially wealthy, for few Thai farmers get rich from their toil on the land, but they were able to offer very generous quantities of food to the monks. After going out on binderbaht, the monks would sit down together on the floor of the open-sided sala often with more than 30 dishes of food for breakfast.

Eating was always preceded by a short chant to remind us that we relied on alms round for our food but that the food was merely a requisite or medicine for the body. After breakfast there was another short chant to thank the donors. This chanting never became routine for me. It helped me not to take my food or its availability for granted, as I had done in the past. Food had always come from Sainsburys and the fridge had always been full.

There were a number of very poor landless families in the village and they would frequently come to the sala to share the monks' food, though always politely waiting until the monks had finished eating. Very little food was wasted.

After breakfast, I would spend the rest of the morning in study or trying to learn Thai with Giant or, if I could get out of that, I would disappear into the forest for meditation. My periods of sitting meditation were usually preceded by a short time in walking meditation, (in Thai this is referred to as Jongrom meditation) and I had cleared a path in the undergrowth about 20 feet long and 2 feet wide for this purpose. Before any meditation outdoors, I would first carefully sweep the leaves from around my meditation platform and from the walking path.

There were a few dangerous 'creepy-crawlies' lurking in the forest, scorpions being the most frequently seen and they liked to hide from the sun under the dead leaves. We had one type of scorpion that I was told was extremely dangerous. Locally it was known as an 'elephant scorpion' on account of its size. I had seen them over 5 inches long. They were jet black and shiny with huge claws, like something Sigourney Weaver would pit herself against. I found them fascinating and loved to watch them, but I always kept my distance. I once picked up a broken piece of asbestos in the forest. There were at least 20 'elephants' lurking underneath. We had lots of the smaller green and beige ones too, much less dangerous but still capable of giving a very painful sting.

An old tractor cog wheel was beaten in the sala to announce lunch at 11 am. It made a lovely 'ding' which was perfectly audible even in the forest, though I would often ignore it and continue my meditation. Lunch was usually whatever was left over from breakfast, which was sometimes very little.

I was rarely disturbed in the forest. Acharn Waow had told the villagers that my main purpose in coming to Nahoob was to follow a strict programme of meditation and that I wanted to be as isolated as possible. They understood but because of the natural friendliness and curiosity that is so much a part of the Thai character, many couldn't resist coming either to just stand and silently watch me, or try to talk to me. The villagers of Nahoob were all descended from Laotian people and spoke a weird mixture of Thai and Laotian wrapped up in a very local dialect which I couldn't understand at all, and nobody has ever been able to understand my atrocious Thai. Communication was impossible and eventually they stopped coming to visit, but we were all on very friendly terms and did a great deal of smiling at each other.

The people were usually extremely considerate towards me whenever I was meditating. My platform was close to a dirt track that ran alongside the monastery boundary, screened by trees, and the farmers would slow down their tractors as they went past that point so that the engine noise would be less disturbing to me.

I think some of the villagers, especially some of the old ladies, found me very strange and were perhaps a little frightened of me. Although rural Thai people usually have a great deal of respect for monks who practice meditation, they are often quite wary of them, believing that meditation helps develop supernatural powers and attracts spirits or ghosts to be near the monk. Although this is entirely untrue, at least as far as I know, it did help keep people away from the forest.

I tried to spend as much time as I could in the forest though frequently, like everybody else, I had to help with various simple jobs around the monastery. I very much enjoyed sweeping leaves, using a broom made of very slim slivers of bamboo. Some of our trees had leaves more than a foot long which would drop off and quickly dry and curl in the sun. Sweeping them up became a form of mindfulness meditation. I was mentally 'watching' the movements of the body and hearing the sound of the broom against the leaves and so on.

Sometimes all the monks were invited to a house for breakfast or lunch but this was much less frequent than at Wat Mahadhatu, which suited me. Occasionally we also had to go to other nearby monasteries to take part in ceremonies that required a specific number of monks. Although most of the local monasteries were large in area, they were generally home to only a few monks, so we all had to help each other out.

At 5 pm each day I had to ring the bell again for evening chanting and by about 6 pm was ready to spend the rest of the evening in study, meditation or in trying to memorise the chanting. Most days followed much the same pattern and many days were spent in silence. Quite frequently I would not say a word for several days, except for morning and evening chanting. There was no vow of silence, but even the Thai monks rarely spoke to each other unless there was absolute need.

There seemed to be little idle chatter, no gossip between us: there just didn't seem to be much that needed to be said. I was glad about that. Like many Westerners and I suppose people everywhere, I had talked far too much in the past, often using a conversation simply to get my own opinions across. Conversation was just another way of massaging my own ego. At Wat Nahoob we all got on with our own practice in our various individual ways and felt little need to talk about it. It was the time for silence and contemplation.

Chapter 14

Strangely enough, the one person I did regularly 'talk to' was a farmer who couldn't speak English at all and who couldn't understand my Thai. It was a decidedly odd relationship but one which he seemed to enjoy as much as I certainly did. The farmer's name was 'My', but in common with all the villagers he had the prefix 'Yom' if being spoken to or referred to by a monk.

Yom My was in his early 40s, married and with several children. He owned only a little land and his house reflected his small income. I think he earned about £600 a year from his rice crop. The house was really just a shack but he made me most welcome there on several occasions. As a child, he had been a temple boy at the monastery, then later a novice and then, for a short period, a monk. His life revolved around Wat Nahoob and he was very helpful to all the monks, especially to Acharn Waow, to whom he was of course related in some obscure way.

We communicated initially with the aid of a couple of dictionaries I bought, a Thai-English version for him and an English-Thai for me. Additionally we would both enthusiastically draw little pictures to try to illustrate what we were trying to say. Yom My amazed me with his ability to remember English vocabulary and although he never particularly wanted to learn English with me, he was keen to try to communicate. He had had little formal education as a boy but was extremely knowledgeable about the birds and animals, the seasons, and the plants and herbs that grew around the monastery. He had endless patience in trying to explain things to me and over the months our communication gradually improved as we each began to know which words the other had learned.

Sometimes he would come to see me late at night, often after a whisky drinking session. He would apologise profusely for his near-drunken state and bow most respectfully, though usually I had to help get him upright again. I would lecture and wag my finger at him and threaten to give him the Five Precepts, but all in a very good-natured way.

One day he and his wife, Yom Noi, asked me if I would like to go on a picnic to the mountain. Yom My also explained that there was something he wanted me to see, though he wouldn't say what. I said 'yes' to the picnic immediately for at every breakfast or lunch at Nahoob, we were always surrounded by villagers who seemed especially fascinated to watch me eat. I got used to it, but I longed for a meal alone. This was due partly to my shyness at being constantly watched, but also because there is a form of mindfulness meditation concerned with eating which I liked to practise sometimes but which requires every action involved in eating to be done slowly, which is not at all suitable for a group meal.

Early in the morning on the day of the picnic, Yom My and Noi came to pick me up in their tractor. This was a delightful machine which was little more than a mechanical buffalo cart. At the front was a two-stroke engine and two small wheels, then seven-foot-long handlebars which acted much like reins. These were joined to a two-wheeled cart with a high seat for the driver. They are extremely versatile machines, for the wheels can be changed to heavy corrugated metal grips for working in the mud of the paddy fields, or to road wheels. The cart and rear wheels can also be 'unhitched' and various strange bits of farming equipment can be attached to the front to make a hand-held motorised plough. On the road they are neither particularly comfortable nor fast and the journey to the mountain took about three hours, though it was great fun for me. I very much wanted to drive the tractor but Yom My was rather shocked at the idea.

We skirted past Wat Khao Nor and continued driving along the base of the mountain, which is entirely encircled by a fairly good road. We eventually came to a halt under a huge old Bo tree surrounded by massive half-buried boulders that had crashed down from the mountain many years before. The whole of the base of that part of the mountain was covered in a bamboo forest and it was a delightfully cool, shady and silent place. The only sounds were bird calls and the cries of monkeys high up on the mountain.

Yom Noi laid out a tablecloth on the ground under the Bo tree and then 'pracaned' the food to me. This is a respectful way of passing food to a monk. It must be done with two hands, bare-footed and followed by a graceful 'wai'. They had gone to a great deal of trouble to cook and pack food that they were sure I would like, nothing too spicy, no fish and plenty of fruit and vegetables. After all this was presented, they left me alone, for monks and laypeople do not eat together. They wandered onto the mountain to pick bamboo shoots for their evening meal and I didn't see them again for several hours. In fact, I didn't see anybody at all for several hours, for not a single car or tractor passed by on the road.

I had my very slow meal in perfect peace and it stands out in my mind as one of the most successful mindfulness meditations I have ever practised. After the meal I chanted quietly and then settled under the tree to practise sitting meditation. Unfortunately I had eaten rather too much and fell asleep almost immediately. I didn't wake up for a couple of hours when Yom My and Noi came back down the mountain. I told Yom My that we should be heading back to the monastery because the journey was a long one and I had to ring the bell for evening chanting. "Mai bpen rai", he said, and drew a clock in the dirt to show that we had to stay on the mountain until 6 pm. "Why?" I asked, but he wouldn't say.

We climbed back onto the tractor and drove for a couple of hours to a very desolate part where the mountain had a great piece missing from one side. A little track turned off from the main road there and led us to a wilderness of gigantic boulders and stunted trees. Yom My told me that the mountain had collapsed at that point many hundreds of years ago. He finally stopped the tractor. It was about 5.45, the air had cooled and there was a slight breeze. We sat in absolute silence. I didn't know quite what was going on.

What I was to see may be very common in Thailand and all over the world for all I know, but I had never seen or experienced anything like it before. At a few minutes before 6 pm all the birds, insects and monkeys suddenly fell totally silent. This instant ceasing of every sound was extraordinary. I really felt quite strange. If there had been any hair on my neck, I'm sure it would have stood up. There was a definite tension in the air, as though something was about to happen—which indeed it was.

Very slowly a sound started to roll down from the top of the mountain. Almost inaudible at first, it quickly built up until it was a very loud hissing ululation, so loud that Yom My couldn't hear me when I asked him what it was. It rose and fell quite distinctly and it wasn't just a sound, it was also a *vibration* that could be felt as a tingling in the air and on the skin and it was coming from inside the mountain, almost as though the mountain was breathing. Suddenly it stopped. For perhaps a minute there was absolute silence on the mountain, then the eerie sound started again, built up, and stopped. It went on like this for about ten minutes and each time the sound was just a little louder and the silence between a little shorter.

Yom My silently and rather dramatically pointed to a narrow fissure about 400 feet up on a perfectly sheer rock face. I watched, but at first there was nothing to see. Quite suddenly, what I thought could only be thick black smoke started to pour from the fissure, but it didn't behave like smoke. It was like a great black snake, twisting, turning, coiling back on itself and writhing in the air, but in a consistently wide and dense 'tube' about 15 feet across. It was bats, literally millions of them; so many I thought the mountain must be entirely hollow. And they didn't come out in a great mass, They came out in an orderly line that never seemed to vary in its width.

Soon this twisting column of bats stretched for perhaps 20 miles or more across the countryside and only then did the leaders start to fan out. The front of the column became a widening and indistinct haze in the distance. The bats continued to pour out of the fissure for about 15 minutes and then, quite suddenly, the column came to an abrupt end, with not a single straggler. Yom My told me it happened every day at exactly the same time. He said that as far as he knew the cave, or cave system, inside the mountain had never been explored: the fissure was inaccessible except to the most professional of rock climbers.

Our journey back to Nahoob was exhilarating for it started to rain slightly, much to Yom My's and Noi's discomfort but to my great delight. I love the rain but Thai farmers only like it when it falls on their crops and most Thai people seem to loathe getting wet, especially on their heads. The sun was setting behind Khao Nor and although I had long since ceased thinking of the mountain as 'magical', I was delighted to know that it did in fact hide a secret.

The rain got heavier. Yom My looked at the sky. "The rainy season is coming", he said.

Chapter 15

Before the start of the rainy season, monks must decide on both the monastery and the kuti they will stay in for the duration of the Pansa period. On the day Pansa starts each monk must chant a determination in his kuti that he will not move to another until the three-month period is over.

When I had first visited Wat Nahoob and meditated in the clearing in the little forest, I had sat in the centre of a group of four trees. They weren't particularly old trees, each was only about 20 feet high, but by some accident they formed an almost perfect square, each side about fourteen feet in length. The two at the 'front' faced Khao Nor and each had a branch growing from about halfway up its trunk. These branches curved upwards and towards each other, making a beautiful Gothic arch shape. The topmost foliage of the trees made a roof over the space beneath, keeping it shaded at all times of the day. I thought at the time it was a delightful place but I would never have imagined that one day I would have a little 'house' on that exact spot.

When I returned from England and moved to Wat Nahoob I stayed in the main kuti block with Acharn Waow, Giant, Phra Maha Pern and another monk whose name I never knew. I was perfectly happy there and thought I would live there for the Pansa, so I was quite surprised at breakfast one day when the abbot announced he was going to have a kuti built for me in the monastery grounds. Its size, style and location would be entirely up to me, he said.

After breakfast we all walked around the grounds, together with the village carpenter and an assortment of other villagers. But of course

I knew exactly where I wanted the kuti to be—in the centre of the four trees. I imagined something about twelve feet by twelve feet which would not only be large enough for my needs but would also fit into the square neatly. No good, explained the carpenter. Whatever size the kuti was to be, we had to allow an additional three feet all round for the roof to overhang as a protection during the rainy season. He indicated with his machete that it would be no problem to chop the trees down. No, I said, that wouldn't be necessary. We would simply reduce the size of the kuti together with the overhanging roof until it could fit into the square. I had to settle for a room about nine feet square but that was perfectly adequate for me and my few belongings.

We all squatted in the clearing and with a stick I drew a design in the dirt of how I envisaged the kuti. There's really not a great deal one can do with a building only nine feet square and the final 'plan' showed it to have a window in each side, each window had two wooden shutters, and a door at the front which was to face the mountain. It would be on three-feet-high concrete legs. There would be four or five wooden steps and the roof would slope from the front to the back. I particularly wanted the door to be at least six feet high so I could stop banging my head. The ceiling had to be high enough for me to raise my arm to get my robe wrapped around me. The abbot approved all this but also suggested we should add mesh windows and a mesh inner door as a protection against mosquitoes and other insects.

The conversation then got into the practicalities of building the kuti and I wandered off a little to observe the scene. There were about a dozen people in the clearing; monks and villagers, squatting on the ground and all chatting animatedly. Each one had his own idea of how the kuti should be built. I thought how marvellous this picture was; how very Thai. These people did not know me, we could not communicate, they knew nothing about my culture and they didn't know whether I would still be there the next day, but here they were, discussing how to build the Phra Farang a kuti in the forest. Someone was donating the wood, someone else the concrete and the carpenter was giving his labour free. A friend in England once told me she couldn't understand what she called my "curious affection" for the Thai people. Here at least was part of the answer: the Thai 'jai dee' towards strangers .

At that part of the wood, the perimeter of the monastery was only about 20 yards from where my kuti was to be sited and I wandered outside. Parallel to the perimeter trees was a dirt track and on the other side of that an eight-foot-wide concrete irrigation ditch. Beyond the ditch there was nothing but unbroken miles of paddy fields stretching in every direction. Dotted about in the paddies were little wooden platforms on stilts, with straw or palm leaf roofs. These were shady shelters in which the farmers could eat their lunch or take a little nap. Exactly in the centre of my horizon was Khao Nor. The scene was a ground level view of what I had seen from my visit to the mountain. Bright green paddies and sparkling lakes as far I could see. There were villagers working in the fields, each wearing a colourful sarong and a traditional lampshade-shaped straw hat. A lone buffalo tethered to a tree watched me mournfully and silently. The air was clean and fresh; there was no sound of cars or motorcycles and I sat beneath the shade of a palm tree thinking, I *live* here, and I could hardly believe how lucky I was.

Over a period of a few weeks the kuti slowly took shape. It looked like a cross between a little Swiss chalet and a rather grand garden shed. It was perfect. Inside it was clean and dry and smelled sweetly of the mango wood which had been used for the floor boards. It was spacious enough for me to live simply but comfortably and to undertake my nightly meditation. I could not use my outdoors meditation platform very successfully at night because the mosquitoes, moths, bats and other flying things were a very big distraction, though strangely I don't think I have ever been bitten by a mosquito in Thailand.

When the kuti was almost complete, the village electrician arrived with his bag of cables, plugs and switches. He wanted to know where I wanted the fluorescent light fitted. "But I don't want electricity", I told him. "I'm going to have candles". He looked at me as though I was quite mad and went off to report to the abbot his failure to connect me to the mains. Soon afterwards Acharn Waow came to see me and asked why I didn't want electricity. Candles would be sufficient for the simple life I wanted to lead, I explained, and would he allow me to have the stumps of last year's candles which I had seen in the Bote. These candles are usually about six feet tall and about nine inches thick and are made to burn throughout the Pansa. With a few of the foot-long stumps I was sure I would have ample light to see by.

In fact, this was a stupid piece of vanity as I realised later and I'm sure the abbot realised immediately. I was already seeing myself as the old forest monk, meditating and studying by candlelight and probably writing my notes with a quill pen too. The abbot smiled and said that of course I could have the candles.

On my first night in the kuti I sat surrounded by five blazing candles and it was like sitting in the middle of a bonfire. The candle flames were fully seven inches high and the temperature inside the kuti was unbearable. It was also extremely hazardous, for my robes were hung on a rope stretched across one wall and I was flapping about in my sabong in constant danger of setting both myself and the kuti on fire and I still didn't have enough light to read or write by. On the first night I got a headache from the flickering light and blew the candles out to go to sleep. The kuti was immediately filled with smoke and fumes from the smouldering wicks. I had to sit outside in the forest for a while to let the air clear, feeling an absolute idiot.

A few days later, the abbot asked me if I was sure that I didn't want electricity. "Well, OK", I said, "if it pleases Acharn". We both smiled.

Soon after that I not only had a fluorescent tube on the ceiling, I also had a spot lamp, an electric fan, a kettle and a small stereo to listen to my chanting tapes. So much for the ascetic old forest monk. Never mind, I was now ready for my first Pansa.

Khao Pansa, or Vassa, the three-month rainy season retreat, was an established practice in India long before the time of the Buddha. At the beginning of the rainy season, monks and ascetics of many religious philosophies would take up residence in a particular place and stay there until the wet season had passed. There were practical reasons for this, for much of the low-lying land was flooded and what roads or tracks existed were frequently washed away.

When the Buddha established the Sangha, there was no prohibition against his monks continuing their wanderings during the monsoon period. This worried some of his disciples who asked him if it was right that ascetics belonging to other schools stopped travelling during the wet season whilst: "Sakyaputtiya Samanas (Buddhist monks) go on their travels alike during winter, summer and the rainy season, crushing the green herbs, hurting vegetable life and destroying the life of many small things". The Buddha agreed that it was not right and told the monks: "I prescribe, O bhikkus, that you enter upon the Vassa"*.

The purpose of the Buddha's decree was not just so that monks would cease damaging crops but also that they would have a fixed period for study, meditation and to teach newer monks. Although in modern times monks could travel regardless of the weather and without damaging crops, the tradition of the Pansa as a period of study and reflection remains.

We were to have five men ordain for the rains retreat. Three of them were about 20 years old, that being the minimum age at which a man may become a monk. They had been born in the village but, like so many of its young people, they had left Nahoob to find work in the cities. The other two ordainees were older men who lived in the village and they ordained a few weeks before the rains retreat started.

The three young men returned to Nahoob about a week before their ordinations to discuss the details with Acharn Waow and their families. Acharn Waow was an Upachaya so he would be conducting the ceremony himself. He decided they should all be ordained at the same time on the same day—the day before the start of the Pansa.

Never having seen a rural ordination before, I thought the triple ceremony would be much the same as mine in Bangkok, a quiet, sober and sombre affair. I was quite wrong, for although the ceremony itself was exactly the same as mine, the build up to it was anything but quiet and sombre—and it certainly wasn't sober.

The day before the ordinations, lorries started arriving in the village with marquees, chairs, tables and sound systems with speakers so large I thought maybe Iron Maiden or some other heavy rock band had included Nahoob on a world tour. Although Thai people usually conduct their daily lives in a quiet way, they have a natural exuberance and an ordination party is a good excuse for making a lot of noise and letting off a great deal of steam.

The night before the ordinations, the noise from the village was deafening and nobody got any sleep. Everybody in the village was celebrating and they were still at it when I dragged myself up the bell tower at 3.45 am supposedly to wake everybody up. From my vantage point at the top of the tower, the village looked wonderful—almost Christmassy. Every house and barn, and even many trees, were covered in flashing fairy lights! The ordinations were to be held directly after the monks' breakfast and the festivities continued up to the very moment that the three young men were carried over the Uposatha's threshold.

Just as I had walked from Section 5 of Wat Mahadhatu, so the three ordainees walked from their family homes in the village. Each was newly bald and wearing the white net robes but they also had net veils over their faces and carried flowers, looking exactly like blushing brides, but without the expensive hairdos. Each walked to the hall under a huge red, white or gold umbrella carried by a family member and when they reached the hall each was hoisted onto the shoulders of friends for the triple circumambulation.

The three processions entered the monastery grounds from different directions and every inhabitant of the village was in one procession or another. They were accompanied by friends and supporters who had come from Bangkok and the other cities where the young men worked.

Unlike my orderly procession with the silent nuns, these were each preceded by what might loosely be called a percussion 'band', each with a mobile 'Tannoy' system. The purpose of the bands seemed to be to make as much noise as possible and to compete with each other in the decibel stakes. It was not until I had attended many such ordinations that I realised that the noise they were making actually had a tune. I came to think of it as the 'Ordination March'. At the time it seemed to bear no resemblance to music as it is known anywhere else in the world and I think I would have preferred Iron Maiden.

The three processions were timed to reach the Bote at the same moment, but the bandsmen had started banging away at their drums and bashing their cymbals at different times, with the result that there was the most hideous cacophony of noise, accompanied by women wailing at the tops of their voices and everybody 'ramwonging' away like mad. The ramwong is a traditional dance involving a graceful weaving of the body and arms while walking or moving in circles, but it wasn't graceful on that occasion when many of the dancers were not only hungover but falling over. The dance had dropped any pretence of elegance.

From my vantage point high up on a balcony that circled the Bote, I watched as the three ordainees and the hundreds of supporters circled the hall three times. They were all going in the same direction, thank goodness, and carefully stepping over fallen fellows who were flat on their backs but still managing to ramwong. It was bedlam, but everybody was so happy and many looked up at me as they passed and smiled or 'wai-ed' at their Phra Farang. I smiled back, happy to be their Phra Farang; happy and proud to be part of that important day in Nahoob.

The next day, right on cue, the rain arrived.

* From Max Muller, 'Sacred Books of the East'. Mahavagga 111.

Chapter 16

In Europe we think we have rain, but until I experienced a tropical rain storm I really had no idea of what it could be like. When the rain hit Nahoob it seemed to be almost solid water falling from the sky. On the occasions when I was caught out in it, I had to hold a hand over my nose, otherwise breathing was actually difficult.

Within a few minutes of the start of a rain storm, rivers, streams and lakes would appear in every depression and hollow. The wells overflowed, the irrigation ditch overflowed and unfortunately the toilet cess-tanks overflowed. If the rain was accompanied by high winds, which was usual, coconuts would fly through the air like cannonballs, and on one occasion killed one of the temple dogs.

During a storm one night, a fifty-foot-tall coconut palm tree fell over, missing my kuti by only about twelve feet and bringing several other young trees crashing down all around. A tree fell across the roof of the main kuti block directly above the abbot's bedroom, causing extensive damage to the roof but happily none to Acharn Waow.

If the downpours were accompanied by thunder and lightning they were especially dramatic, particularly at night. The inside of my kuti would be brilliantly lit by the almost continuous flashes as though it was daylight, and the concrete foundations would actually shake with the reverberations of the thunder. I thoroughly enjoy storms, but if a storm was directly overhead, I was sometimes both awed and a little scared of the incredible forces that were hurling themselves around me and sometimes, it seemed, directly at me.

My kuti was on a slight rise and as the rain increased in intensity and frequency through the three-month-long season, I gradually became surrounded by a lake which crept nearer to my steps each day. Through the lake swam black and green snakes, some six feet long, in search of the bull frogs that had appeared in their thousands and which kept me awake at night with their throaty calls.

As the water rose, every creature living in the vicinity seemed to take refuge under, above or in my little ark. A wild cat moved into the gap between the roof and the ceiling where it had a litter of kittens. The mother would peer and hiss at me from her refuge in a most unfriendly and ungrateful way and I feared that one day she would pounce on me from the roof and rake her claws across my bald skull. My kuti started to smell very badly of dead things and I sent Yom My to climb one of the trees to see if there were the remains of dead animals in the cat's lair. He was most reluctant but anyway got nowhere close enough to see, for a great paw with what appeared to be titanium-plated claws appeared at the gap, ready to do battle in protection of the little ones.

A lovely little squirrel-like animal appeared one day in a downpour and made a dash into the roof gap, which was rather a bad choice of refuge considering the cat-from-hell was living there at the time. I never saw the squirrel again.

A twelve-foot-long boa constrictor hung around beneath the kuti for a few days. It was sick, having been captured by a villager in the paddy fields and brought to the monastery in a very large stone water jar. The villager had caught it with a looped cord and the loop was tied tightly just behind its head, which I think must have made it difficult for it to breathe or eat. I have no particular fear of snakes and when it first arrived at the monastery I put my hand into the jar, to the horror of the on-looking villagers, and cut what I could of the cord away, but I couldn't get all of it.

The snake stayed in the jar for a few days and then, to my delight, escaped one night. It was seen a few times around the monastery and I kept track of its movements. It smelled horrible and I guessed it must have been suffering badly from the constricting cord, but I couldn't get close enough to it to cut the knot. I knew that boa constrictors killed their prey by crushing with their coils, but I hadn't realised until I had my hand in the jar that they also have teeth, very big ones and lots of them, so I was a little more wary of it. Finally it arrived under my kuti and just lay there, apparently too sick to even move and I guessed it was safe to approach it. I cut the cord without difficulty. I very much hoped the snake would stay around but after a few days and presumably after a few bull frogs, it slithered away into the paddies.

Although I am not frightened of snakes I did move pretty quickly when a cobra slithered up my kuti steps and poked its head around the partially open door. Yom My told me there were also king cobras in the monastery grounds. I never saw one, but just before I moved to live at Nahoob, a local woman was bitten by a king cobra and died.

Sometimes I found twelve-inch-long, bright red millipedes on my steps and even in the kuti itself. I believe they are quite dangerous. There were also scorpions everywhere, looking for somewhere dry to spend the night. I discovered that although the plank walls of my kuti were snake-proof they were definitely not scorpion or great-big-hairy-spider proof and these creatures were frequent refugees from the rising water.

I am both fascinated and terrified of big spiders and I really don't want them anywhere near me. I acknowledge their right to live: somewhere else. They were extremely difficult to shoo out with a coconut-hair broom and I sometimes spent hours looking in every nook and cranny for one that had escaped my wild swishing, but I could never relax if I knew there was one anywhere in the kuti. On one occasion, I woke up in the morning on my floor mat to find a saucer-sized spider sitting on the floor only inches from my face, sort of throbbing at me. Even though I knew these spiders were not dangerous, I leapt straight up into the air with a childish scream of terror, but the spider was even more terrified and fled.

As the paddies flooded, so the monastery grounds became overrun with land crabs. They look much the same as the ordinary English seaside crab, rather dull and about four inches across, but they had an enormous claw and I'm sure could give quite a nip. There were thousands of them and we had to be very careful when walking about at night to avoid treading on them. Unfortunately I did once, quite unintentionally, and it was a most disgusting feeling, though I'm sure more so for the crab than for me.

I found a small bat hanging in a corner of the kuti, which was a great surprise for there seemed no particular reason for it to be there, rain or no rain; Khao Nor was probably only a few minutes flying time away. It was very beautiful and I very much wanted to hold it, but I thought it might be sick. Believing that bats can carry rabies, I avoided that corner for a few days. The bat suddenly dropped off the ceiling one evening, stone dead. I burned its little carcass in the forest.

A sort of flying ant caused the biggest problem during the rainy season. Every time it rained, literally thousands of them would find their way into the kuti. They would fly around for a while and then their wings would drop off and they would crawl about on the floor. Soon after they would die and the floor could be almost covered with their bodies. Occasionally I could sweep up a whole bucketfull of them in one evening.

Often it would be raining when we went out on binderbaht. Monks do not use umbrellas during almsround and we would trudge through the village on dirt tracks six inches deep in slithery mud, our sodden robes clinging to our shivering bodies. It actually didn't bother me; in fact I rather enjoyed it, much to the disbelief of the other monks, who absolutely hated it.

Like everybody else, I suffered with continuous colds and bronchial infections throughout the rainy season. My kuti was constantly damp, as was my bedding, books and all my robes. I shivered, shook and sneezed my way through the three months, until the day came when I thought I was *really* ill.

I began to experience an ache around the top right-hand side of my chest and under my right arm. It wasn't particularly bothersome at first but it slowly got worse and after a few days, I discovered that all that area was covered in small red lumps. The lumps themselves were neither painful nor itchy, but they seemed to be hot.

Yom My came to visit me and I showed him the lumps. He recoiled in horror at the sight and said in his most dramatic English stage voice: "It's the .... it's the ...Lerm!" Oh God, I had the Lerm and I was going to die. From the look on Yom My's face I would probably take the rest of the monks and the entire population of the village with me. But what is the Lerm, I asked, and what does it do?

Our communication skills didn't extend to medical terms so he drew a picture of a very thin torso, my torso, on a piece of paper. Then he added spots to one side. He looked at me enquiringly. Yes, yes, I understood so far, I said, get on with it. Then he added more spots until they travelled all the way across the chest. Then he turned the piece of paper over and continued drawing spots until they had entirely encircled the paper. When all this spot-drawing was finished he looked at me with a very sad expression. "Dead", he said.

This rang a distant bell in my mind. When I was about six years old my mother had been quite ill and it was something to do with spots or lumps on her stomach. An unkind neighbour had told me that if the lumps circled my mother's body and joined up, my mother would die. I seemed to remember that my mother had been suffering from shingles, but wasn't it an old wives' tale about the sufferer dying if the lumps joined up? I had no idea. I looked up 'shingles' in my dictionary. Well, I certainly didn't have small pebbles lying in masses along a seashore, but if one took pebbles for lumps and the seashore as my chest it was actually quite a good definition of what I seemed to have.

What was I to do? I asked Yom My. He indicated rather belatedly that I wasn't to worry and that he would fetch a doctor and off he went. I was lying on the floor quietly dying and working out how many hours it would take for a doctor to come from the nearest hospital when within minutes Yom My returned, accompanied by a very old man carrying a plastic shopping bag with a picture of Father Christmas on it.

I had seen this old man in the village a few times but I hadn't known he was the local shaman. Many Thai villages have these 'doctors', well-versed in Animism, folklore, massage and herbal medicines, but I had never seen one work before. They are frequently highly respected and consulted on all sorts of matters, not just medical problems.

I would actually have preferred a paramedic team, but since the old man had been kind enough to come out in the pouring rain, I smiled my most grateful and bravest smile and turned myself over to his ministrations.

The doctor looked at my chest, then he looked at Yom My. Some sort of understanding seemed to be pass between them, as though to say, "It's hopeless, but we'll try". Nobody spoke. The doctor rummaged in his plastic bag, probably for his stethoscope, I thought, but instead pulled out a very prickly foot-long cactus. "Yar", said Yom My solemnly. Medicine. And what, I enquired nervously, was I supposed to do with it? "Boil it", said Yom My. Well, that was a relief. And then I was to drink the liquid, I supposed. "No, no", said Yom My, as though he had never heard anything so ridiculous in his life. I was to make it into a poultice and smear it on the lumps. But first the doctor would give me the main treatment.

The doctor made three very rheumatic but very respectable bows to me and then held my right arm straight up. He started mumbling a chant, but I could not recognise the language. It wasn't Thai, or Laotian, or Pali, perhaps it was a combination of all three, but it had a definite 'flow' and he certainly wasn't making it up as he went along. This was a deadly serious charm he was weaving and his old face was screwed up in concentration.

After a few minutes the charm had been cast and then, much to my surprise, he suddenly blew into my armpit. I nearly burst out laughing but thought that would be entirely inappropriate and kept my face as serious as possible. Yom My heaved a sigh of relief. I thanked the doctor who, apart from the chanting, hadn't said a word. He bowed again and Yom My helped him back to the village.

Word spread quickly that the Phra Farang had the Lerm and over the next few hours a stream of villagers came to wish me well, wish me goodbye or blow in my armpit. I wasn't sure if a monk should let ladies do anything quite so intimate but they seemed to think it was respectable so I let them get on with it.

Later that night as I lay miserably stinking of boiled cactus, I heard footsteps coming along the forest path. That was unusual because at night especially the villagers avoided my part of the forest like—well, like the plague really. They believed it was haunted even before I arrived. Yom My occasionally visited at night but I could recognise his footsteps because they were broken up by drunken falling-over noises. To my surprise my night caller was one of the village lads, a boy of about 16 who sometimes came to my kuti in the daytime with a bunch of his friends to try and teach me rude Thai words on the pretext that they were very polite and should be used often. His name was Rabbit and it turned out that the shaman was his grandfather.

Rabbit had brought me a small pot of white cream which had obviously come from a hospital. There was a big scoop out of it but the pot was still half full. "Yar", said Rabbit. Yes, but what was it for, I asked. He said I was to apply it to the lumps and assured me that they would be gone in a few days. I asked where the ointment had come from and it then became clear why the boy had come to my kuti so furtively. The year before, he had suffered with the same symptoms and his grandfather had taken him secretly to the hospital. No cactus poultice for the shaman's grandson! Rabbit asked me not to tell anybody because his grandfather would lose 'face' in the village.

I showered the evil-smelling green gunk from my body and applied the white cream. Within a couple of days the lumps and aching had entirely disappeared. Was this due to the cactus, the cream, or the very sincere chanting and arm-blowing? Maybe a combination of all three? I really don't know.

I also don't know what the disease was called, but it wasn't the Lerm. Some time later, when my Thai vocabulary had improved a little, I discovered that 'lerm' is Thai for 'forget'. Yom My had said "It's the ... it's the ... I forget!" Well, it remained the Lerm to me and I suffered no harm and I had had a fascinating glimpse into Thai rural life.

Chapter 17

Although Acharn Waow was consulted by the villagers on any matter of importance the ordinary monks didn't usually have much contact with them except during 'cycle of life ' ceremonies. The most frequent of these during the rainy season were funerals. The wet season and the following cool season usually bring an increase in the number of deaths in rural areas, especially amongst old people. Fairly elaborate rites are involved in Thai funerals, though in the very poor northeastern region I have seen bodies carried into a field and burned on a pile of wood with the minimum of ceremony. I think this is probably less frequent now that most villages are close to a monastery with a crematorium.

At Wat Nahoob we had a new crematorium which had never been used, but it was to see a very great deal of use during the rainy season. At that time it seemed that almost every week one of the village patriarchs or matriarchs passed away. When families are bereaved anywhere in Thailand they try to do the best they can for the deceased by 'making merit' on behalf of that person. It is believed that the merit can be transferred to the dead to help him or her achieve a better next life. Relatives and friends of the deceased will almost invariably offer food and gifts to the monks on behalf of the dead person and male relatives will sometimes ordain as novice monks for a few days, or even just for the day of the funeral.

The dead are not usually cremated before the seventh day and occasionally may be kept for much longer to allow as many people as possible to pay their respects. When especially important or highly-respected people die, the body may frequently be kept for 100 days, or even longer, before being cremated.

In rural areas, the body is usually kept in the family home and each morning nine monks are invited to take breakfast there. The monks chant for about half an hour and after breakfast, chant a short Pali verse about the impermanent nature of life. This verse translates as:

'Alas, transient are all compounded things. Having arisen, they cease. Being born, they die. The cessation of all compounding is true happiness.'

This verse is chanted while the monks hold a length of 'sacred' white cotton string called 'sai-sin', which passes from a Buddha image and is attached to the coffin. I understand traditionally it is believed that this string helps the dead person continue contact with the suttas and blessings being chanted on his or her behalf. On each of the six evenings preceding the cremation, four monks will go to the house to chant passages from the Abhidhamma, their faces hidden behind ceremonial fans. Although these passages and all the other suttas and blessings are chanted in Pali the Thai people are well aware of their meaning and they genuinely seem to help the bereaved in their grief.

The first time I was invited to take breakfast at the house of a bereaved family in Nahoob I stood in absolute amazement at the sight that greeted me. The family were quite poor and the house was little more than a large ramshackle shed on stilts, but it was like walking into an Aladdin's cave of colour and light.

In the main room was an enormous three-foot-deep, rectangular, wooden coffin, painted white with masses of gold plastic decoration. It was set on a stand about five feet high. This was surrounded by dozens of brilliantly coloured 'bouquets' of huge, polystyrene flowers and wreaths made of towelling folded into the shape of peacocks and butterflies. A photograph of the deceased person stood on a stand at one side and in front of the coffin on a small table was a brass bowl containing a single huge incense stick and two candles. Everything, including the coffin, was covered in flashing fairy lights and the whole display was back-lit with green neon.

The room was quite small and contained not only the coffin and accessories but also a 5-piece brass and percussion band, the nine monks and dozens of villagers. As villagers arrived at the house, each would approach the coffin and knock a few times on one end. We ate our breakfast sitting on the floor with the eight-foot-high flashing coffin towering over us while the band played a very mournful dirge.

Although I found it quite bizarre, it was not at all undignified. The lights and colour were, I think, a reflection of the Thai people's 'healthy' attitude to death. It is a time for grief but the family try to make the atmosphere as bright and cheerful as possible because it is not necessarily an unhappy time for the deceased who, hopefully, is on his or her way to a better life.

On the seventh day of that particular funeral, I and several other monks went to the house to escort the coffin to the monastery's crematorium. It is an old tradition that the dead should not leave the house by the normal route, however, since it is usually impractical to hoist the coffin through a window, the stairs are sometimes covered with cloth or banana leaves to make the usual route a little different.

Once down the stairs, the coffin was loaded onto a traditional buffalo cart that had been beautifully repainted in black and white. This was pushed and pulled along the dirt tracks by some of the village men. Most of the mourners wore black, white or a combination of the two. The procession was headed by the band, then came a villager scattering rice grains along the path. He was followed by members of the immediate family who carried the photograph of the dead person and one of the giant incense sticks. The monks followed in single file, each of us holding on to a long length of very thick sai-sin which passed through all our hands to the coffin, though we were not actually pulling the cart. Behind us came half a dozen men and little boys who had ordained as novices for the day, then the rest of the family and friends, all holding the sai-sin.

When we arrived at the monastery we were joined by other monks who had been invited from nearby temples and we assembled on a high wooden platform which had been erected in one of the salas. I don't think there is any specific number of monks traditionally required to perform funeral rites: I have been present at a funeral with only a few other monks but also have taken part in a ceremony which involved more than a hundred. It seems quite common to have the same number of monks as the deceased person was years old: 50 for a person who was 50 years old, for example.

Acharn Waow gave a 30-minute talk about death and impermanence and the monks chanted briefly, after which we were each presented by the chief mourners with a sabong, an incense stick and some white wood shavings which had been beautifully worked into the shape of a rose. After the chanting, the whole congregation proceeded to the crematorium where we escorted the coffin three times around the building in an anti-clockwise direction. Unlike the functional and discreet crematoria of Europe, Wat Nahoob's was really quite colourful and pretty. It was on a high concrete base with steps on three sides, which led up to a small chamber with a tall thin chimney. Like most temple buildings, it was painted white with lots of red and yellow cast concrete decoration of 'heavenly beings' and with snakes and scrolls in every angle. On top of the newel posts were large, pink concrete lotus buds. Most Thai crematoria that I have seen are of similar style, though some may be considerably larger and grander.

The coffin was unloaded from the buffalo cart and carried up the stairs where it was dismantled to reveal an inner plywood box. This was placed on a stand in front of the oven. The inner box is frequently left open if the sight of the body is not likely to cause too much distress to the family or, perhaps, is not too badly damaged.

When everything was in place, the immediate family members placed sabongs on top of the body and a number of monks were invited to take them from the coffin whilst chanting the same Pali verse about impermanence. This tradition recalls the time many centuries ago when monks in India would use bits of cloth found in charnel grounds to make their robes. The rest of the monks then mounted the stairs and placed their incense sticks and wooden flowers in the coffin on top of the body. Friends and family followed to do the same while the new novice monks scattered coins into the crowd, symbolising the dead person's final rejection of materialism.

The inner coffin was then loaded onto a metal trolley with wheels, quite a bit like a wheelbarrow. In the mesh bottom of this were layers of newspaper, cardboard, wood and charcoal. These were lit and the trolley was rolled through the crematorium's heavy steel door. The door had a small peephole so the village 'funeral director' could check on the progress of the cremation. There was also another small hole through which he could insert a long, forked, metal rod to shift the position of the body from time to time.

Beneath the chamber was a trap into which ashes and small fragments of bone fell. These were collected by the family the next day and would be kept in a small brass urn, a miniature of the huge stupas and chedi that can be seen in many Thai monasteries. The urn would be kept in the family home, together with the photograph. Many homes I have visited have had dozens of such urns, together with photographs going back many generations lining the walls.

Although some of the rites seemed strange to me, basically all people face the same practical problem or duty when a death occurs in the family; to dispose of the body. The Thais seem to do it with more ritual and ceremony than Westerners, but it also seems to be done in at least a semi-cheerful way. It has always been my impression that the moment the oven door is shut, the grieving stops and life for everybody else goes on. There has always seemed to be a calm and pragmatic acceptance of death; a natural understanding that this is how all lives end and that tears and hand-wringing aren't going to change a thing. I have only very rarely seen anybody cry at a funeral in Thailand. I think this pragmatic attitude shows a very profound understanding of the Buddha's teaching about the impermanent nature of all things. At the same time this attitude is also at least partly responsible for the Thais ability to enjoy themselves on a moment-to-moment basis, without worrying too much about what the future might hold. There is only one certainty in this life, and that is its ending.

I know that some of the rites and rituals I am involved in are purely Thai culture and are more closely related to Animism and Brahmanism than to Buddhism. At funerals at least that doesn't cause me any personal conflict as a Buddhist monk. I believe *anything* that helps people in their time of grief must be worthwhile, whether it be the fairy lights or the Pali chanting.

Funerals for monks follow much the same pattern as those for laypeople. During my rainy season at Wat Nahoob, one of our monks died and was cremated at the monastery. Just before the Rains Retreat started, an old monk had wandered into the monastery and asked Acharn Waow if he could spend the Pansa with us. The abbot had said he could. The old monk, Phra Ghin, was more than 80 years old and had been a monk for about five years. His village was in the northeast of the country but he had spent several years wandering all over Thailand, staying each night in any temple he found himself close to and the Rains Retreat in any temple which would accept him.

Phra Ghin seemed to be a very nice but rather lonely old man and I would occasionally sit with him in the forest. He would chatter on in his Laotian dialect and although I rarely had more than a vague idea what he was talking about, I would smile, nod or shake my head, whichever seemed most appropriate.

He started to complain of stomach pains and after a few days Acharn Waow sent him off on the back of a motorcycle to Nakhon Sawan hospital, about 40 kilometres away. About a week later he died and was returned to us wrapped in polythene in the back of a pick-up truck.

Because he had been a monk, only other monks were allowed to prepare the body for cremation. Most of the monks disappeared rather hastily and Phra Maha Weera and I got the job of dressing the corpse in Phra Ghin's robes and laying it into the coffin. I had never handled a corpse before and I thought I might find it distasteful or at least distressing, but I didn't, even though the dead flesh smelt very bad.

I found I was totally able to accept that this was no longer the Phra Ghin I had known, however slightly, and the corpse had no personality at all. It seemed no different from the occasion when I had found one of the temple dogs dead and had dragged it into the woods to bury.

When we had the corpse laid out in the coffin, Phra Maha Weera placed a single lotus flower on the chest and carefully folded the cold hands around it. To me that was very touching and at that point, much to my surprise, I found I had a lump in my throat, though I had previously been quite emotionless.

We covered the corpse with Phra Ghin's spare robe but before we nailed the lid down, Yom My appeared with a very thorny branch he had cut from a bush. He laid it on top of the body. This, he told me, was to prevent Phra Ghin getting out of the coffin in case he came back to life in some sort of zombie state. This is an old Animist belief that still seems to be very accepted amongst rural people, though Yom My seemed quite embarrassed to admit it.

Acharn Waow had informed Phra Ghin's family and we delayed the cremation until they could arrive from the northeast, after which they took the ashes home with them. Life carried on as usual at Wat Nahoob and I don't think I ever heard Phra Ghin's name mentioned again.

Although Thailand is frequently known as 'The Land of Smiles' it can also be a very violent country, as one particular week at Nahoob was to show.

The week started off with the news that six people had been killed at the end of the track when their pick-up, driven by a drunk, crashed into a tree. None of the dead actually lived in Nahoob so that didn't concern us too much.

A few days later there was another death. There was a man living at the monastery who occasionally helped out around the grounds. He was generally considered 'good for nothing' and I rarely saw him sober. He was very unpopular in the village and I really don't know why the abbot put up with him—compassion, I suppose.

I was woken up at about 2 am one morning by a monk banging on my door. I couldn't make any sense of what he was saying but it was obvious he wanted me to go with him to the sala. I followed him and found a small group of villagers standing around the body of the man. He had been shot through the chest by his brother-in-law following a drunken argument. It was a very messy corpse because the bullet had exited through the back and had made a very large hole indeed. I was told that the police had already been and gone and that they had confiscated the gun. Money had changed hands and that was the end of it. We cremated the body the next day with the minimum of ceremony and most of the village people attended in what I can only describe as festive mood.

In the same week we were sitting in the sala eating breakfast surrounded by villagers when a man rushed in and blurted out what was obviously exciting and dramatic news, for all the villagers hurriedly left. The monks continued eating without comment and I was totally mystified as to what had happened.

It turned out that a village woman had cut her husband's throat with a machete. Why I never knew, and I never knew the outcome, but it was cause for another quick and discreet cremation.

Chapter 18

Because I lived at Wat Nahoob for more than a year I was able to observe and sometimes participate in most of the annual Thai festivals, both religious and cultural.

Thai people love to celebrate. In rural areas their celebrations are perhaps not particularly 'sophisticated' by Western standards. Some very loud music, lots of simple food, alcohol and plenty of friends and neighbours dropping in are all the ingredients necessary for 'sanuk' — fun.

The Thai calendar is full of special cultural and religious dates and almost every month seems to bring an excuse for people to get together, either for making 'merit' at the temples or simply for having a good time.

My personal favourite at Nahoob was Songkran, the Thai New Year festival which is celebrated over three days in mid-April. Since 1941 the official New Year date has been January 1, but Thai people still celebrate the traditional period with considerably more enthusiasm.

Mid-April is actually a very logical time for farming people to celebrate a new year because it comes at an important change in the seasons: the ending of the hot, dry weather and the theoretical beginning of cooler and wetter weather (though in fact, the rain may still be some months away). The change in the environment at about that time is considerable. It is much like the change in Europe from winter to spring when new leaves and buds start to appear on dry and apparently lifeless trees and shrubs.

Originally Songkran was very much concerned with the anticipation of rain and included Brahmanic rain-invoking ceremonies. It is still all about water—throwing it over everything and everybody. To walk down any street in any city, town or village in mid-April means getting wet; perhaps a few drops of water poured over the hands, a bucket-full poured over the shoulders or a total soaking with a hosepipe. Monks and royalty excepted, it doesn't matter who you are or what you are wearing, you are expected to smile wetly and join in the fun. For three days, everybody is constantly dripping and the amount of water used must run into millions of gallons.

The idea of cleansing out the old year and welcoming the new is also observed in the home when a good 'spring clean' is undertaken and everything is prepared for the new beginning. House parties go on for days and almost every province has a parade through the city streets, with school bands, floats and, a recent addition, a Songkran Queen.

Many people will also go to their local temple where the main Buddha image is given a ritual washing as each person pours a little water onto it from a small silver bowl. Traditionally people may also take clean sand to the temple to spread around the grounds.

I was at Wat Buddhapadipa in London getting my knee repaired during my first Songkran as a monk. The festival has no particular significance in Buddhism but the monastery allows the grounds to be used for celebrating Thai cultural festivals. On that day, there were many thousands of visitors enjoying displays of Thai classical dancing, Thai boxing and a wide range of Thai food from a market that had been set up in the temple car park.

The main Buddha image in the Bote was too big to be moved but a smaller image was set up on the marble steps leading to the Bote and this was ritually washed by many hundreds of people.

The monks also got a ritual washing. We all sat on our mats in the shrine room in the house with our hands held over small silver bowls. Dozens of laypeople filed past on their knees and each poured a few drops of scented water over our hands. Very reverential and restrained and not a bit like the celebrations at Nahoob the following year.

At Nahoob, the village people celebrated in the monastery grounds and visitors from miles around came to join in the festivities. These included a band playing traditional northeastern or Laotian music amplified to ear-splitting volume; at the same time an outdoor movie screen showing a Chinese kung fu movie also at ear-splitting volume, much eating and drinking and some graceful and gradually not-so-graceful ramwonging. Everybody was madly throwing water about but frequently the recipients were too far gone to even notice.

Of course, the monks didn't take part in any of this (and I think Acharn Waow closed his eyes to the amount of alcohol being consumed in the monastery) but towards the end of the afternoon the temple bell was rung and the monks assembled in front of the Bote where a line of chairs had been set up on the grass.

I was expecting much the same as I had experienced at Wat Buddhapadipa but when country people celebrate, they do so with great enthusiasm and within seconds I was soaked from shoulders to feet.

Hundreds of people filed past in two lines, one in front and one behind the chairs, and absolutely drenched us from cups, buckets and a hosepipe. As the temperature was in the 90s this was quite enjoyable for me, even when several of the children slipped ice cubes down the back of my robe. For about 45 minutes we sat while gallon after gallon of water was poured over us until our chairs started to sink in the mud.

The Thai monks accepted all this with unmoving expressions, keeping their eyes fixed firmly on their folded hands. But Thai happiness is infectious and how can one ignore hundreds of excited, smiling faces? I couldn't and within seconds I was smiling back at them, exchanging a sincere 'sawatii pee mai' — Happy New Year — with each person that passed in front of me and occasionally flicking water at faces I recognised.

By the end of the day, the lawn was a quagmire and everybody was sodden, but the people had really made the most of it and I think I enjoyed it almost as much as they did.

At the other end of the year in November is the Loi Krathong festival which is also concerned with water but quite different from Songkran.

A 'krathong' is a small boat, usually made from banana leaves, and 'loi' means 'to float'. The little boats are usually circular and about nine inches across. In the centre each carries a candle, an incense stick, flowers and sometimes a small coin.

In Nahoob on the day before Loi Krathong, I sat with some of the village children and watched for hours while they made their little boats. Like most Thai people they were extraordinarily gifted with their hands, deftly bending and shaping the leaves and flowers and carefully folding and mixing tiny petals into complex coloured patterns. I had a try but my krathong was quite hopeless.

Some krathongs are considerably more elaborate and may be several feet across and in height. Many cities hold competitions between schools, businesses and institutions to see who can make the best looking krathong.

The origins of the festival are obscure. I have read that it comes from or was inspired by similar ancient festivals in India and China but also that it originated in Sukhothai in about 1300. One explanation for the festival is that by making offerings of light, incense and money to the river spirits, the sins of the donor are carried away with the krathong. Another explanation is that the gifts atone for boating or swimming over Buddha images which may be lying on the river bed. Yet another explanation is that it prevents death by drowning.

The festival has no place in the religious calendar, so I was quite surprised when a group of teachers from a local school came to the monastery to present me with a krathong they had made. It was beautifully decorated and at first I thought it was a cake. On closer inspection the decoration proved to be hundreds of red, yellow and green chilies. That evening I joined some of the village people at the monastery pond, carefully lit my candle and gently launched the little boat. There were several dozen krathongs moving lazily on the pond in the night breeze, each with its candle flickering and being reflected in the water.

Later that evening, I and several other monks went into Banpotphisai town, to the Ping river, and watched many hundreds of krathongs of all sizes bobbing past on the strong current. The town was packed with people, most carrying krathongs. Many shops were open for the sale of 'ready-made' krathongs, many of them, sadly, made from polystyrene. There were bands and parties on every street corner and in the grounds of the main temple, Wat Somciel, a concert and film show were running simultaneously and the monastery itself was brightly lit with thousands of fairy lights. As monks, we had to keep a distance from the festivities but it was lovely to see so many people enjoying that special night.

The religious calendar starts in May and the full moon day of most months has some special significance, though only four are widely celebrated. These four; Visakha Puja, Asalha Puja, Khao Pansa and Magha Puja are all national holidays in Thailand.

Visakha Puja in May commemorates the Buddha's birth, Enlightenment and passing away. According to some scholars, and using the solar calendar, Prince Siddhattha was born on 18 May AE 68, became the Buddha on 20 May AE 103 and passed away on 15 May AE 147. Many people go to their local temple on the night of Visakha Puja to take part in a 'wien tien' — a candle-lit procession which circles the Bote.

At Wat Nahoob the monks assembled on the high balcony of the Bote at dusk to await the arrival of the villagers. They came in procession from three different directions and each person carried a candle, flowers and incense sticks. They joined us on the balcony and, with the monks in the lead, we circled the Bote clockwise three times. During the circumambulation, the monks began to chant softly and this chanting was taken up by the villagers. After the third time around, the candles and incense were placed in holders around the balcony and we entered the Bote to pay our respects to the image there.

The ceremony only lasted about 30 minutes but it was very beautiful. Afterwards, as I walked back through the forest to my kuti, I looked back at the Bote, it looked quite dazzling, lit up by hundreds of tiny points of light.

Asalha Puja is in July. It commemorates three important events: Prince Siddhattha's renunciation of his princely life; his first sermon as the Buddha and the coming together of his monks three months after he passed away (the First Council). July is also the beginning of Pansa, the Rains Retreat, when many young men ordain for a few months.

There was an incident in the Buddha's life when he left his monks and, tradition says, lived alone in the forest with only the animals to care for him. This occasion is remembered in September and at Wat Nahoob the sala became a forest for the night, with whole cut banana trees tied to the pillars and representations of monkeys and elephants lurking in the shrubbery. Throughout that night until dawn, the abbot read stories of the Buddha's life to about 50 villagers. He read from a high pulpit that had been fantastically decorated with tiny flowers woven into curtains resembling lace.

'Wan Ork Pansa' signals the end of the Rains Retreat and on that day the laypeople make special offerings to the monks. At that time many young men who ordained just for the Pansa, disrobe (although some stay as monks for another month) and in the village the celebrations went on through the night as families welcomed their sons home.

In the period between the full moons of October and November, the 'Tot Kathin' ceremony takes place. A kathin is a wooden frame on which cloth is stretched for cutting and sewing. At the time of the Buddha, the kathin was used by monks who had to make their own robes from scraps of cloth found in charnel grounds and forests. Now however, the occasion has become a time for laypeople to present new 'ready-made' robes to monks who have completed the Pansa.

Magha Puja in February is an important festival. It marks the occasion, about three months before the Buddha passed away, when

1,250 Arahants spontaneously gathered together without previous arrangement. All these Arahants had become monks on the invitation of the Buddha before the introduction of the lengthy ordination service. Then the Buddha would invite a person to join his following simply by saying 'Ehi-passika' — "Come and see". It was at this spontaneous meeting of the Arahants that the Buddha recited the Ovadapatimokkha (the rules of the monks) and announced that he would pass away within three months. Magha Puja is celebrated in much the same way as Visakha Puja, with a 'wien tien' procession.

All these festivals, both cultural and religious, were enjoyable to me, but I found myself becoming increasingly involved in other ceremonies which sometimes seemed inexplicable. Although I didn't understand them, they didn't worry me particularly at first. When a pick-up truck arrived at the monastery to take us to someone's house for breakfast or lunch I just got in and went along with the crowd, usually not having the faintest idea of where we were going or why. But slowly, and unknown to me at the time, a doubt was beginning to form — shapeless and nameless, but gently simmering away at the back of my mind....

Chapter 19

Doubt, according to Buddhism, is one of the major obstacles to spiritual progress and understanding*. We must face our doubts, examine them, understand them and clear them away before we can continue our progress.

Before I ordained as a monk, I frequently travelled around Thailand, usually staying in monasteries and taking every opportunity to observe religious services and customs. Sometimes I would see an activity that I did not understand and I would always try to find out which aspect of the Buddha's teaching the ceremony was concerned with. When I once asked a very senior English-speaking monk about the relevance of the sai-sin, the 'sacred string' and the realities of 'transferring merit' to dead people he told me, "It's Buddhist metaphysics". Often the ceremony didn't seem to be concerned with Buddhism at all. "It's Thai custom" was frequently the answer to my questions. At the time, I accepted that it was all part of the 'richness' of Thai Buddhism.

When I actually had to be involved in some of these ceremonies as a monk, that was still my attitude—at least at first. Although I couldn't see the relevance of some of the rituals, that didn't mean they weren't right; they seemed perfectly harmless and at the time I gave them little conscious thought. I had no strong opinions but very slowly and quietly I was becoming uneasy and later began to question whether I really ought to be involved at all. Some of the ceremonies seemed quite bizarre to me.

In my first week at Wat Nahoob, all the monks plus others from another near-by monastery were invited to take breakfast in a field.

A pick-up truck arrived at the monastery early in the morning and we were trundled along miles of bumpy tracks and then cross-country to a paddy field where a small three-sided blue and white marquee had been set up. Inside the marquee was a makeshift platform for the monks. It was about three feet high and it looked exactly like a stage for a very amateur dramatic performance. Sitting expectantly in front of the stage were about 50 people, most from a nearby village.

The nine monks climbed a step onto the stage and I really felt as though we should break into a song and dance routine. Instead the other monks chanted for about 30 minutes and we were then presented with breakfast.

Stretching all around us were miles of paddies with not a single tree in sight, except one: a very tall palm tree about ten yards away. This tree, it turned out, was the reason we had been invited to the field. It had apparently been struck by lightning, though I could see no sign of damage, and the farmer wanted it 'blessed'. After breakfast, Acharn Waow unrolled a length of sai-sin, one end of which was tied to a small Buddha image and then round a bowl of water. A beeswax candle was fixed to the rim of the bowl and the wax dripped into the water. The string was passed through all our hands and the other end was tied around the tree. We chanted briefly and the abbot splashed the lustral or 'holy water' over the tree as well as over the audience. We were each presented with a small gift of money and a flower and driven back to the monastery.

On another occasion, a man drove into the monastery in a huge cattle truck. It was new and the owner wanted it 'blessed', presumably so that it wouldn't break-down or crash. After a bit of chanting, Acharn Waow used his finger to daub a symbol on the bonnet with white paint and then liberally splashed truck and driver with lustral water. We were all presented with a gift of money and the truck driver, no doubt convinced of his invincibility on the roads, drove off happily at high speed. The truck would probably never be taxed or insured but at least it had been 'blessed'.

I have been with a chapter of monks when we have carried out a similar ceremony on a new motorcycle and once on a whole fleet of trucks and pick-ups. There were many such occasions, sometimes several times each week, but one of the most bizarre for me was when we were invited to take lunch at a house in order to 'bless' a new washing machine. The head monk painted some symbols on the machine and splashed it with water while the rest of us chanted holding onto the sai-sin, which was tied around the machine.

This was exactly what the householder had wanted but I came away (clutching my envelope of money) feeling distinctly uneasy, the words 'hocus pocus' uppermost in my mind. What exactly was I doing—and why? From where, or from whom, I asked myself, did our 'power' or authority come to enable us to dispense 'blessings' on trees, trucks and Hotpoint washing machines? Was I a Buddhist monk or was I becoming a Brahmin priest? And yet I had seen photographs of the Supreme Patriarch, the head of the Thai Sangha, performing exactly the same type of ritual on a new aircraft. If the Supreme Patriarch, whom I respected as much as any Thai monk, performed these rites, who was I to question or doubt them?

I had even been present at an 'exorcism'. I was not a monk at the time but I watched as a chapter of monks chanted whilst holding the sai-sin, one end of which was tied to a Buddha image and the other to the corner of a large white table cloth. The cloth was draped over a woman who lay on the ground writhing and screaming. I have also seen the white cloth used for a couple of people who simply felt they were going through unlucky periods. I was quite willing to accept that if the 'exorcism' or the ceremony for the banishment of bad luck actually worked for the people involved, if they really believed they had been exorcised of their demons or bad luck, then it had some validity. But was it Buddhism? Was it even 'Buddhist metaphysics'? Or was it just superstitious rubbish?

This wasn't criticism of Thai Buddhism, for one cannot criticise or praise a thing until one knows for oneself absolutely that it is wrong, or right. And even if I found these rites and rituals were not strictly Buddhism as I understood it, I still would not have any criticism for the way Thai laypeople practised their religion. That was entirely up to them and I had no right to say 'You should practise in this way, or that way'. The laity of all faiths take from their religion whatever they personally require of it to suit their particular circumstances and frequently add to it for the same reason. But can this be valid for Buddhist monks? For them, there can be only one way of practice, the way the Buddha taught. That, presumably, was why we had become monks, so we could follow that teaching. Any doubts I had were reserved for the way we, as monks, were practising, and more specifically, for the way I seemed to be expected to practise.

I have often seen very senior monks blowing on the heads of young sickly children. Their parents seemed to believe this would cure the child. What the parents chose to believe is up to them, but do the monks who indulge in this sort of practice also believe they have miraculous or spiritual healing powers and can cure sickness with their breath? Maybe they had, I just didn't know. Even I had been stopped on the street and had been presented with a spotty baby and had been asked to blow on its head.

I knew of course that every country and culture has its superstitions and traditional beliefs. In England, there are old wives' tales about black cats, walking under ladders and pinches of salt, that sort of thing, and possibly some of these superstitions stem from pre-Christian pagan religions, just as many of those in Thailand stem from old Animist beliefs. That's fair enough and I believe they add 'colour' to the culture of the people. But we were Buddhist *monks* following what I had always considered to be the most scientific and logical of religions; a religion based on wisdom, not on superstition.

I recalled a story about the Buddha. He was speaking to a group of people who were confused about the conflicting religious philosophies they were hearing from various teachers. They asked the Buddha for his opinion. Although the Buddha's reply was concerned specifically with religions, it seemed to me that his advice could be applicable to many other situations as well. He said: "Do not be led by reports, or tradition, or hearsay. Do not be led by the authority of religious texts, nor by mere logic or inference, nor by considering appearances, nor by delight in speculative opinions, nor by seeming possibilities, nor by the idea 'this is our teacher'. But when you know for yourselves that certain things are unwholesome, wrong and bad, then give them up.... And when you know for yourselves that certain things are wholesome and good, then accept them and follow them".

I didn't *know* for myself that these 'blessings' and the paraphernalia that went with them were wrong, or at best, merely empty rituals, but they simply didn't seem to fit in with what I *did* know. They didn't feel right, that is, they didn't feel right for me, but no doubt they felt right for the laypeople involved. They were simple and harmless little ceremonies, but they seemed to be the only thing the people demanded from the religion and from the monks. They were planting seeds of doubt in my mind. Not about Buddhism, but about what Buddhism seemed to have become.

These were not just the opinions of a new, know-nothing monk, for several of Thailand's most senior and revered monks were saying or writing much the same thing. In, I think, his last book before he died, Acharn Buddhadasa had written that Thai Buddhism had hit 'rock bottom'. Another greatly respected Thai scholar monk, Dr. Phra Maha Chanya wrote in his book 'Introduction to Buddhism': "The role of the Buddhist monk is being changed from the holders of Dhamma light to performers of rites. They change their role from spiritual leaders to civil servants. No one can deny that the majority of Buddhist monks give the people what they want even if it sometimes contradicts the real Buddhist truth".

I was once present at a lecture when a very senior monk was telling junior monks how they should behave in front of laypeople. The lecture was in Thai but was translated for me sentence by sentence. The senior monk said: "It is the monks' job to know how to chant and to be a good actor in front of the laity". Was it? Were we, then, merely *pretending* to be monks? Acting out a part in our costumes and chanting our lines and blessings for the benefit of the paying audience? Is that why the Buddha had set up the Sangha all those centuries ago? Is that what I had given up my life in England for?

I was hardly conscious of it at first, but my sense of sabbai was disappearing and I found myself becoming increasingly cynical and unhappy. I decided to push all such thoughts aside. That was a mistake. The seeds of doubt had taken root and were to come to fruition in a most dramatic way.....

* Doubt is one of the 'Five Hindrances': 1. Lustful desires; 2. Ill-will, hatred or anger; 3. Sloth and torpor; 4. Worry and restlessness; 5. Sceptical doubts.

Chapter 20

I have not often been really angry in my life. As a child I was prone to what my mother called 'temper tantrums' and I think in my mid-teens I was a bit sulky, always claiming that nobody understood me. In adulthood, I had frequently given a show of anger but the emotion had rarely been very deep and was always soon forgotten. I don't think I really knew what true anger was, until one day at Wat Nahoob I suddenly and unexpectedly found myself in a rage. It was an emotion of a depth and completeness that I had never experienced before. It blinded me to all reason and later led me to question whether all my hundreds of hours in meditation, seeking some understanding and control over my mind, had been a waste of time and whether my apparent developing equanimity was a thin veneer.

The howl of a dog started it. At Wat Nahoob, we had half a dozen fairly mangy dogs that hung around looking for scraps. Most dogs seem to have a hard time in Thailand, especially in rural areas, for they are not generally seen as 'pets' in the same way that Westerners view their dogs. Even if someone ties a piece of coloured string around a dog's neck, thereby claiming ownership, the unfortunate animal may still be subjected to abuse.

There was a man living at Wat Nahoob who had, I think, been there for many years as a sort of general handyman. He was 'educationally disadvantaged', not his fault, for his parents had been too poor to provide any sort of education for him at all and he had never been to school. He had grown up as a temple boy in a series of temples, unable to read or write, but despite his academic failings, he was quite well-liked in the village for his apparent knowledge of herbal medicines and traditional Thai massage. I thought he was a bit strange and the village children told me he was 'ting-tong', I think the equivalent of 'barmy' rather than clinically mad and they seemed not to like him and tended to stay away from him, though it was some time before I understood why. He usually had a lovely smile on his face and I certainly didn't dislike him, though we could not communicate in any way.

His sister, who lived in a nearby village, offered to sponsor him as a monk so she could 'make merit'. He ordained and built himself a tumble-down shack in the forest about 50 yards from my kuti, whilst waiting for his sister to have a more permanent structure built. His nearby presence caused me no problem at all but I did start to find myself becoming disturbed by his treatment of the dogs.

When it came to dogs (and, as I later observed, small children) he seemed to have a vicious and bullying streak in him. Frequently I would see him beating a dog, or even a tiny puppy, with a bamboo cane, or firing stones at the dogs with a catapult. At these times his 'lovely smile' seemed to turn into an ugly and perverse leer. This sort of behaviour is not particularly unusual in Thailand, even in monasteries, but I always tried to ignore it. I reminded myself constantly that I lived in a society where many attitudes were different from my ingrained Western ones and that I should not use my personal values or conditioned responses to become judgemental about other people.

One day I was sitting on my kuti steps reading, when a dog howled in pain. The sound of a dog being hurt had become fairly commonplace in that part of the woods, but that particular howl was quite different. It was a scream of agony. I looked across at the monk's kuti, for I knew he had to be the cause. He had one of the old male dogs tied down to some sort of bench and was castrating it with a machete. Any ideas I may have had about remaining aloof and non-judgemental disappeared in an instant.

I made no conscious decision about whether I should be involved or not, in fact my mind didn't seem to be functioning on any level.

I only recall that I suddenly arrived at his kuti and somewhere in my blind dash along the way, I had uprooted a sapling that I now held in my upraised hands above my head. I brought it crashing down across the monk's back. The machete went flying into the bushes somewhere. I don't know if I was making any sound at all but if I was, I doubt if it would have been heard above the dog's howling and the monk's screams of outrage. I seemed to have no control at all and continued to beat him about the head and shoulders. I wanted *him* to know what pain was and I'm sure if the machete had still been handy, I would have castrated him so he would know exactly what it felt like.

Although my anger seemed to totally consume me, it probably lasted no more than a minute or so and was snuffed out as quickly as a candle flame. One moment I was in a rage and in the next it had totally disappeared. I was left trembling uncontrollably and the sapling dropped from my hands to the forest floor. The monk lay on the ground staring up at me in fear and shock. I just stood, trying to control my trembling body as well as my mind as full realisation of what I had done swept over me, almost causing me to faint.

At that moment the dog was forgotten, the beating was forgotten, the man at my feet was forgotten. I was horrified and I watched my faith and belief in myself as a monk, a *meditative* monk and a follower of the Buddha's teaching, evaporate. I was left empty and desolate. I had neither learned nor understood anything. It all suddenly seemed to have been a waste of time. I turned and walked slowly back to my kuti.

I was able to put the dog's agony out of my mind easily, for the deed was already done and there was nothing I could do to correct it. I did look for the dog in the monastery grounds that day to see if I could care for it in any way but I couldn't find it, I never saw it again. The monk suffered no damage and later the same day was telling the other monks and villagers about the Phra Farang's extraordinary behaviour. The incident had already become a joke for him. In fact, I had broken an important Vinaya rule by attacking another monk, but that didn't bother me too much. Whether I had done right or wrong was not my immediate concern and I felt no particular guilt about the attack itself. It was all secondary to what then seemed to be the main issue.

What was the main issue? I had, probably for the first time in my life, totally lost control, something I had never even done *before* I started my meditation studies. How was it possible? I had to find the answer.

I meditated hour after hour, day after day. In my kuti... outside in the forest... walking... sitting... standing... lying down... getting absolutely nowhere. I tried using mantras: Bud-dho ... Om Mani Padme Hung. Nothing. I tried counting the breaths... I watched the breath at the nose tip... I watched the abdomen rising and falling. It was all a total waste of time. Although my rage had completely disappeared, a new anger was growing inside me like a tumour. I could find no reason for it. I could hardly eat and was sleeping only a couple of hours at night. I became more and more frustrated and slipped into deep despair. My thoughts even turned to leaving the monkhood.

On about the seventh night after the incident, way past midnight, I left my kuti and walked through the dark and silent monastery grounds to the Bote. The building was always kept locked, though the key was left lying on a ledge just outside the door. I let myself in, pulling the heavy door shut behind me. I stood for a few minutes just inside the door, in total darkness and silence, wondering why I had come here. There was nothing here, I told myself; it was just a building with a big bronze image of a man who had died centuries before. There was nothing here to console me; nothing that could help me understand my own feelings; there was no refuge here from my anxiety and confusion. There was no Buddha here.

I walked slowly to the alter. I lit the two candles that had been placed there earlier in the evening in preparation for morning chanting next day. They did little to lighten the darkness of the small hall but they faintly illuminated the larger-than-life sized image on its plinth about five feet above me. The white enamel eyes, half closed, reflected the light and seemed to stare down at me.

I lit three incense sticks and carefully placed them in the brass, sand-filled container between the two candles. The fragrant smoke drifted upwards in the warm, still air catching the candlelight and flowing around the image.

I knelt on the floor, sitting on my heels, simply looking up at the image. I made no bows. I wasn't at all sure what I was doing there or what I expected to find. Any answers could only be found on the inside, in my own mind, not here in this building, nor anywhere else.

I felt overwhelmingly lonely, close to tears of despair and yet there was some comfort in simply looking at the image. I realised how much I loved and respected this man and everything he was, everything that he became. I felt in some ways that I had not only let myself down but I had also let him down. He had devoted most of his life to teaching the *Way*, teaching people like me. But I hadn't really listened. I had listened with my ears but not with my heart.

It was childish and illogical, I knew, but at that moment I didn't want him to have been just a man, I wanted him to be God. I *needed* him to be God. I needed a cosmic shoulder to cry on. I didn't have the strength to "be my own refuge", as he had taught. I needed something else, someone else, to whom I could bow down to and pray: from whom I could beg for help, or guidance, or forgiveness or sanctuary. I didn't have the courage or strength to travel this path alone.

For a time, I wallowed in self-pity. Tears quietly flowed and I let them flow, continuing to stare up at the image. I stayed there for a long time, several hours. I hadn't made any conscious decision to meditate but I seemed to be slipping in and out of meditation almost naturally, as though it was beyond my control. The tears stopped and I felt the concentration level of my mind increasing, building-up to a degree of focus that I had never experienced before. The self-pity evaporated: the need for a God evaporated; even the concept of 'Buddha' evaporated; only the teaching remained.

The admonition of every meditation teacher I had ever known or read constantly passed through my mind: "Let go... let go... let go. That's all there is to it. Just let go..."

Watch the emotions arising, bring them into full consciousness, observe and examine them dispassionately, see their ultimately delusory nature and let them go.

It all came slithering to the surface. I saw my earlier rage and realised it was just a front; an easily recognisable emotion obscuring much more complex issues. I saw beyond the anger, to my disappointments and frustrations. I saw the ill-will that those emotions had generated. I saw my doubts and I saw an intense and bitter resentment. And there lay the cause of my earlier outburst. Not resentment against the dog-beating monk in particular; this was resentment on a much bigger scale that just happened to condense into that man.

I resented Thai Buddhism. That was the truth of it. I had no resentment against the Thai people at all, but I resented that the culture had seemed to have changed—had been *allowed* to change—the teaching of the Buddha in its original purity. Over the centuries, the teaching seemed to have been undermined, subtly changed and had become so tainted, so corrupted, that it was now frequently hardly recognisable.

I resented what I saw as Thai Buddhism's 'non-Buddhist' practices—the Animist and Brahmanist rites and rituals, the chants and magic charms, the 'sacred' string and 'holy' water. I resented what seemed to be its superficiality and the constant emphasis on 'making merit'. It was good action perfectly in keeping with the Buddha's teaching, but 'making merit' seemed to have come to mean only making gifts to the monks or monasteries. I resented that there seemed to be little effort by most monks to teach the laypeople at more than the most superficial level, as though the Thai people were too stupid to fully understand. And I resented the empty and hypocritical blessings from so-called 'holy men'; men whose secret behaviour sometimes made a mockery not only of the Vinaya but of everything the Buddha taught.* I had been a monk for only a short time, but as a layman I had stayed in dozens of temples all over Thailand and I had seen for myself.

Before I ordained, I had thought the rites, rituals and superstitions of Thai Buddhism were merely 'icing on the cake' and that beneath the icing, the real teaching of the Buddha remained intact. But I was beginning to suspect that Thai Buddhism was all cultural icing and had no 'cake' at all.

I believe the Buddha taught the perfect philosophy and presumably all other Buddhists believe the same. If we, as Buddhist monks, accepted that his teaching was perfect, how could we allow even superficial changes to it? If it was perfect, it could not be made better, it could only be made less than perfect and therefore something different from what the Buddha taught. Was Buddhism enriched by these rituals and superstitions, or was it degraded?

All this resentment and doubt was writhing inside me like a venomous snake and I knew I could never make any personal progress as a monk, nor in my meditation, while such feelings existed. I didn't really know if my doubts had any solid foundation and, even if they did, I knew I could do nothing about the situation. Perhaps at some time in the future, if I was ever skilled enough and understood enough, I would be able to teach Dhamma myself, but such a time was a very long way off.

But, I asked myself, if I resented Thai Buddhism so much, why did I live in Thailand? Why not just take myself off to some other country where I wouldn't *see*? Because the country wasn't a problem, the people weren't a problem. I was a Buddhist monk and therefore, as far as I was concerned, I should be able to live and practise what the Buddha taught anywhere and I certainly wasn't going to run away from the country and people that I loved just because their way of practice was often not the same as mine. My resentment had little or nothing to do with the people, it was concerned with our practice as monks.

But I also recognised that although I genuinely felt that Thai Buddhism was a little 'off course', my own thinking in the matter was possibly equally so. I wanted everything to be perfect in my little world; I wanted everybody to practise the way I thought they should practise—wasn't there some ego here as well? Was I perhaps subconsciously thinking of other monks: "You don't practise correctly, therefore I am better than you"? This needed deep investigation, but I had to face it. It was not something I could run away from. One can run away from conditions, but not from your own mind—that's always right there with you.

After hours of concentrated thought my mind was reeling, but I had to let it all come to the surface. I had to acknowledge and examine my doubts and resentment as dispassionately as possible before I could 'let them go'.

But to realise, to know at an intellectual level, what I resented was not really the issue. Things are always as they are. To resent or approve makes no difference to the conditions themselves. The conditions were not affected, changed or improved by my resentment or anger. Only I suffered. I had to let go of this resentment. Easy to say, but how does anyone 'let go'.

"Just let go ....."

Was letting go the same thing as 'mai bpen rai'—'it doesn't matter'? Perhaps in an ultimate sense, nothing matters, but as a relative truth 'mai bpen rai' was frequently just an excuse for apathy.

The candles had long burned away. I was sitting in total darkness and I felt as though I was faced with a Zen riddle. "Let go". "But how do you let go?" "You just let go" "But how..." The more I thought about it, the more difficult and paradoxical it became. Now my resentment, either as a fact or as an emotion, was no longer the issue. The 'letting go' of it was the problem.

I realised I was actually clinging on to the idea of 'letting go'. This was madness. I had been taught the mechanics of meditation, of letting go, but I didn't know how to do it. Had any of my teachers actually managed it? Yes, one certainly had. The man whose image loomed above me in the darkness. Many of my teachers had spent their whole lives in the robes; studying, practising and teaching meditation. Acharn Amara Thera was probably one of the most knowledgeable meditation masters in Thailand: it was demeaning to suggest that he hadn't taught me anything. But there was actually no way of teaching how to let go; there was no 'method' and there were no words to adequately describe it. It had to be intuitively realised for oneself through meditation, rather than learnt, or taught.

So what had I been doing in all my hundreds of hours of 'meditation'? It hadn't been a complete waste of time because I had learned many things, but I understood now that much of it was of relatively little importance. Yes, through my meditation I seemed to have built up equanimity to a degree and yes, I had worked hard on the other qualities that the Buddha taught should be cultivated; universal love, compassion, and joy at others' happiness, but I saw now that to an extent I had only been fabricating those qualities. They weren't real; they weren't deep. I had, partly at least, been encasing Peter Robinson in a shell. Beneath the surface, much of the old bitterness, frustration, ill-will, anger and petty jealousy, some of which I had never consciously recognised, were still boiling away like a volcano. And like a volcano, they were sure to break out one day, destroying both itself and everything around it. This was no good at all. It had to stop.

I decided to rethink everything I thought I had learned about meditation and to start again. To find my own path. "Look inside", said the Buddha, "for thou art Buddha". Look inside. Yes, I would look inside. I would look as deeply as I possibly could and I would continue looking until I had some answers. Until I *knew* for myself.

The Buddha's final words came to me, as he lay dying under a sal tree in India more than 2,500 years ago. "Bhikkhus, I address you now. Transient are all conditioned things. Strive on with diligence". Strive on. The Buddha himself said that he only pointed the way; it was up to each of us, up to me, to work out my own emancipation; to liberate myself. To strive on with energy, determination and conviction.

Several hours had passed and I was worn out. I was too tired to think any more and I decided to put all this aside for the moment. Now I would go back to my kuti and make some coffee before I had to ring the morning bell. I started to get up from my kneeling position ......

My mind let go.

I actually fell back to my knees. It felt as though somebody had thrown a bucket of clean, cold water over me, not over my physical body but over my mind. For just a moment, my mind seemed to empty itself of all the conflict and rubbish that was in there. Not just of the past week, but all of it, all 40-odd years of it.

I cannot really adequately describe the feeling but for the briefest moment my mind had seemed to be totally silent, totally still, totally *clean* and I had an overwhelming insight into how things could be, how they were meant to be. This was not a 'spiritual or religious' experience, nor any sort of 'enlightenment', it was just a natural result of my practice, but for the briefest moment and for the first time, I saw the potential goal. For the first time I knew what meditation was about.

Like an idiot I tried to hold on to the feeling and of course it disappeared as quickly as it had come. For a while, I continued to sit in the darkness before the darker shape above me. I examined my emotions, poked about in my mind. It was still all there but different, like the sloughed-off skin of a snake. I could recognise the snake from the discarded skin, but the serpent had slithered away. I found I had no anger, no resentment of any kind, just a wonderful sense of peace and of knowing.

I think from that very moment the rites and rituals of Thai Buddhism and the activities of some of the monks ceased to concern me. I realised I was becoming too self-righteous and far too serious about it all. This was hardly the way to develop equanimity! But I saw that none of it really mattered, either relatively or ultimately. How others chose to practise needn't affect the way *I* practised. Each of us must follow his own path. Let it be........

I lit two new candles and three new incense sticks, placing them mindfully on the alter. At some time in the past few hours my robe had slipped off. I carefully adjusted it, sat back on my heels, and intoned three times......

"Namo Tassa Bhagavato Arahato Samma Sambuddhassa".

Homage to the Exalted One. Perfectly Enlightened by Himself.

I bowed three times, with total conviction, and quietly let myself out of the Bote.

The days, weeks and months that followed were to see new energy and determination in my practice. Although it is against the advice of most teachers, I dropped the idea of sitting at specific times of day or for specific periods. I had no 'meditation time' because I did not want my practice to start becoming routine and habitual, something I might take for granted. I meditated instead at the times when I felt it would be most productive for me and sat only until my meditation came to a natural end. Although I was 'determined' I was equally determined that I was not going to force myself to practise if the conditions did not seem right. I would not sit with gritted teeth waiting for the time to pass simply so I could 'log up' more meditation hours.

I actually spent less time in meditation than before but I believe for me it was time more productively spent. I made no conscious effort to regain the seemingly perfect 'emptiness' that I had briefly experienced in the Bote, but I did re-experience it on several occasions, always just as briefly and just as unexpectedly. I tried hard not to cling onto the feeling, nor to actively seek it, but was simply willing to accept that it was one result of my practice.

For a time I thought about leaving Wat Nahoob and going to one of the international forest monasteries where most Western monks live and where conditions, from what I had seen, were more suited to the farang temperament. Forest monks usually follow a stricter discipline than is found in most Thai monasteries and I believe the monks have considerably less contact with laypeople and the ceremonies they need and demand.

But to change my orange robes to the brown of the forest tradition would be only that—a change of outside colour. The 'work' had to be done on the inside and I felt I could do that as well at Wat Nahoob as anywhere else, better in some ways. Although at one of the international forest monasteries, I would certainly find other monks who were practising well and who would be good examples to me, I didn't want to run the risk of subconsciously merely copying someone else's practice. That would only be cloaking myself in outward form. I genuinely wanted to come to grips with the defilements and, in a sense, by placing myself in the more difficult environment of a 'normal' monastery, my defilements and hindrances became clearer and more obvious.

My resentment had been forced to the surface by my religious environment. What I resented was not the issue in the long term. It was the fact that I was capable of any resentment on any issue that needed to be faced and dealt with. To live in a sort of meditative paradise with other Westerners and with little contact with the people would, I felt, be detrimental in some ways to my progress. I decided to stay where I was for the moment (though I did briefly allow myself the vanity of wearing the brown robes of a forest monk!).

My feelings of sabbai quickly returned at Wat Nahoob and the incident of the dog was soon forgotten. Strangely, the dog-beating monk became quite respectful to me after the incident and I never saw him hurt an animal again, so perhaps we both learned something. I began to learn to accept what was going on around me, though not in an apathetic way. Since there was nothing I could do to change things, any action or 'mind-movement' became superfluous and I was determined that my equanimity should become genuinely deep.

The ceremonies, that I sometimes had to be involved in, were undoubtedly frequently Brahmanistic or Animistic in origin but they didn't affect me. They were my duty. They weren't my personal practice. Perhaps that's how many Thai monks viewed them as well. I never capitulated and if I could get out of being involved with them, I would, but that didn't stop them going on. If anything my own practice became better because of them. I started to watch myself much more closely. I constantly looked for signs of wayward practices or the development of 'bad habits'—but I had 'let go' of my resentment.

That's all there was to it really—just 'letting go'.

* My comment refers to a few widely-publicised cases of highly respected monks who have been disrobed in recent years for the most serious Vinaya offences, usually of a sexual nature. The damage they have caused to the Sangha, to Buddhism in Thailand and to the faith of the laypeople is immeasurable.

Chapter 21

As part of Giant's final year at Mahachulalongkorn Buddhist University, he had to undertake social or teaching work in a rural area and that was what had brought him to Wat Nahoob in the first place. He had the idea of starting an English language school for the village children.

Most of the older children in the village attended the local secondary school and although the curriculum included English, the standard was quite poor. This was not necessarily due to the teachers but more, I think, to the prevailing government and social attitudes at the time.

Successive Thai governments had, in theory at least, had an 'equal education for all' policy but in practice the big schools in the cities usually received more financial support and better equipment. Therefore they also attracted the best and most ambitious teachers. Socially and culturally, the majority of children in rural areas, certainly the majority of the boys, were not inspired to break free from their rural environment. Most expected to become rice farmers, just as the male members of their families had done for generations. Some of the girls had quite a different attitude, possibly they had seen enough old ladies permanently bent double from the back-breaking work in the paddy fields and they seemed more determined not to follow the traditional lifestyle.

Even the Thai government acknowledged in the mid-90s that their approach to English teaching had been wrong. The government had stressed the importance of reading and grammatical knowledge and few school curricula included speaking skills. The university entrance examinations did not require students to speak, only to read and write, so most high school teachers had concentrated on those aspects of the language. Even many university graduates had completed their studies with a knowledge of English in theory only. They then had to take private lessons to learn how to converse before they could get a decent job. Most major companies in Thailand now insist that their employees at management level are fluent in spoken as well as written English. I once spoke at length to the head of the English department of a rural secondary school with more than 4,000 students. Receiving just nods and grunts in reply to my questions, I finally asked him how long he had been teaching English. It sounds like a joke, but he looked at his watch and said "Half past twelve". The man had been an English teacher for 16 years and could not hold a conversation.

Giant had it in mind that the school should concentrate on communication skills, my job, while he would teach conversational grammar. The school was to be called rather grandly 'The Wat Nahoob Languages Centre'. 'Languages' was plural because Giant planned that the school would also teach Thai. I would be the only student, albeit a reluctant one.

Giant set up the school in one of the monastery's open-sided salas, with a whiteboard at one end together with desks and chairs that he had borrowed from a local primary school. On 'opening night' we started our lessons to a class of more than 40 students ranging in age from five to 30 years old.

It was very hard and time-consuming work, especially for Giant, because besides giving his own lessons for two hours five nights a week, he also had to attend my communication classes to translate and explain my 'model conversations'.

Most of our students could read very well but few actually understood a word they were reading. I got hold of a text book used in English teaching at the local secondary school and the very limited number of conversational exercises included such useful subjects as 'My holiday in New Mexico' and 'The history of the Apache Indians'. I was really quite appalled. By chance one day, I met a teacher from the school and told her so. Me and my big mouth. It was to lead to having 900 students in my conversation class, though not all at the same time, of course.

Unfortunately the Wat Nahoob Languages Centre was not a resounding success, either at teaching English or Thai. Both Giant and I tried hard but for various reasons, attendance started to decline. Some students stopped coming because they thought learning English would be fun, which we tried to make it, but it was also hard work. Some stopped coming because after spending all day at their regular school, they were too tired to spend all evening in study as well and perhaps they had household or farm chores to do. If it was raining, *nobody* would come, not even Giant. He frequently had to be away from the monastery in the evening for six consecutive nights to chant passages from the Abhidhamma at houses where there was a bereavement. When he was away, I couldn't handle the class on my own because the students and I had little mutual language so I was unable to explain clearly the points I wanted to make.

The school drifted to a close after seven or eight months, but it led to other things. The abbot of the main temple in the district, Wat Somciel in Banpotphisai town, decided to build a school for monks and novices, at which, besides learning the traditional subjects of Pali and Dhamma, the students would also be taught a normal school curriculum. Many novices, some of whom later become monks, are from very poor families and the parents often cannot afford to keep the children at home, so the boys become novice monks. Frequently they have not been educated beyond grade three of high school and sometimes have received no formal education whatsoever.

Teachers of Thai, maths, geography, history and science from various local schools volunteered to give lessons and Giant was invited by the abbot to become headmaster. That meant that he had to move from Wat Nahoob to Wat Somciel. I taught English at his school for a while but my own teaching schedule was becoming so busy that I had to stop.

The teacher to whom I had loudly voiced my opinions about the text book to, came to see me at Wat Nahoob with several of her colleagues. She asked if I would occasionally lecture at her school to fourth, fifth and sixth formers about Western culture, since few of the students had ever met a Westerner before. I was happy to do so but before I knew it, my occasional talk became a weekly event and then turned into a daily conversation class. Finally I was teaching all day, five days a week. At first I didn't mind this at all. It was fun and I have always been conscious that I rely totally on the kindness of Thai people for my food, shelter, robes and everything else in my life, so I was happy to be able to return something to them.

I prepared a teachers' manual which set out what I thought were relevant model conversations for young people. Never mind the American Indians, I based my conversations on typical 'boy meets girl' situations and similar subjects using vocabulary which I thought was relevant and useful in daily life.

As my schedule and work-load increased I found that besides teaching in the daytime, I was having to spend every night preparing my lessons, or giving extra lessons to students who would come to my kuti. I realised I was meditating and studying less and less and at one point not at all. Although on the one hand I was happy to teach, in fact I thoroughly enjoyed it, a more selfish voice inside had started to ask whether I had really given up everything and travelled 10,000 kilometres to live in a garden shed and be an unpaid teacher. I began to question just how far my social responsibilities as a monk extended. By chance, Acharn Amara Thera was in Thailand at that time and I went to Bangkok to see him.

He was quite adamant that I was doing too much English teaching and that my real duty as a monk was only to practise what the Buddha taught and to increase my knowledge of Dhamma and meditation. If I wanted to continue teaching, he advised that I find a 'middle way' between my own studies and my teaching career. I agonised for a long time. I wanted to help my students but at the same time needed to make progress as a monk. Finally the decision was taken out of my hands. The school director decided that English conversation was not a useful subject for his students and that they should concentrate on the requirements of the university entrance examination. My course was dropped.

This decision was to cause something of a fuss at the school amongst the more progressive teachers as well as some of the students, but I was happy to accept the situation. The best students, as well as some of the teachers, continued to practise their conversation skills at weekends at my kuti and whilst talking on a 'one-to-one' basis I got to know some of my students very well.

I was greatly saddened by some of the things I learned about them. All my students were very bright, the brightest at the school, and they very much wanted to continue their education at a higher level. Few of them, however, had any chance of going on to universities or colleges of higher education because of their parents' poverty. Even if they passed the entrance examinations, they would not be able to take up their places. It seemed such a waste, that potential graduates should be forced to work in the paddies or in mundane jobs because of their poor backgrounds. I very much wanted to help, but I had little money of my own left, no income and no way of raising funds to help them.

The top student in the school, Seckson Sukkhassena, was a particularly sad case. He had to live at the school because his parents couldn't even afford his bus fares and one of the teachers was kindly paying his school fees. Seckson wanted to study physics and there was no doubt in anybody's mind that he would easily pass the university entrance examination. Seckson, however, had resigned himself to following a different career. Somebody had offered him a job in a petrol station cleaning car windscreens.

Acharn Amara Thera had made it clear to me that a monk really should not involve himself to any great extent in the affairs of the laypeople, but I was adamant that Seckson should not throw his potential future away.

"No", I told him. "You are going to university". And I was going to London.

Chapter 22

My reason for going to London again was not specifically to seek help for Seckson. I had heard from a friend that my stepfather had suffered a heart attack. After my mother died my stepfather had lived alone and, since he was then in his 70s, I felt I should do whatever I could to help him. Unfortunately I left it too late. Unknown to me he had died about a week before I arrived in England.

It was late February; England was blanketed in snow and it was bitterly cold. For me, coming from the beginning of the hot season in Thailand, the change in the weather was so extreme that I quickly became unwell. I had very little money and could not afford to travel to see my friends, most of whom now lived outside of London. I stayed in the monastery most of the time, helping the other monks and talking with my old friend, Phra Maha Laow.

I was also very happy to meet again some of the Thai and European laypeople who devoted so much of their time in supporting the monks and monastery. During my conversations with some of them, I mentioned that I was now teaching and that I was concerned about the future of one of my students. Within hours of my arrival at the monastery my friends had pledged not only sufficient money to ensure Seckson's university future, but also a surplus to establish a small trust fund* to help others in similar circumstances.

I also had a surprise reunion. The very first time I had visited Wat Buddhapadipa I had met a young man, John something, who told me he was soon to leave England and would be ordaining as a monk in Thailand. I saw John briefly at the monastery a few more times and then not again and I forgot all about him. During that trip to England, John turned up at Wat Buddhapadipa, wearing the purple and yellow robes of a Tibetan monk. We recognised each other immediately and he told me of his time in the orange robes of a Theravadan monk in Thailand.

Many of John's experiences reflected mine exactly and he had reached a point when he had become so disillusioned with Thai Buddhism that he had disrobed. But he had never had any doubts about the Buddha's teaching and he was determined to find a teacher from whom he could learn what he called the 'real' Dhamma. In fact, he had found his teacher in Scotland, at the Samye-Ling Tibetan Buddhist Centre and was now studying Tibetan Buddhism. That was a coincidence because I was also at that time finding an interest in other forms of Buddhism besides Theravada. I had recently been reading a book about Chinese Zen and found it fascinating, though much of it seemed so paradoxical it was beyond me.

We sat in the garden for hours chatting and it was a lovely meeting but I remember thinking what a bizarre picture we must have presented. Me in my orange robes and John in his purple and yellow, sitting on a wall in a snow-covered English garden! I had to tell John, or Dav as he was now named, that I really didn't like his purple shoes very much. He didn't answer, but merely looked at my bright yellow rubber sandals.

Some time later, when I was back in Thailand, Dav sent me a note in which he included a Tibetan 'wishing prayer' about impermanence: .....

"Like stars, mists and candle flames, mirages, dew drops and water bubbles. Like dreams, lightning and clouds. In that way will I view all composite phenomena".

I liked it so much that I found a beautifully-shaped piece of wood, worm-eaten and still with the bark on one edge, smoothed and polished it and asked Giant (whose English hand-writing was considerably better than mine) to paint the words onto the wood. I nailed it over my meditation platform in the forest.

Because I was generally feeling so unwell, I decided to stay in London only a short time, though if I had known how ill I actually was, I would probably have sought medical help in England. I returned to Thailand, happy that I was carrying such good news for Seckson but feeling very ill indeed. Once back in my little kuti at Wat Nahoob, I took an aspirin, went to bed and stayed there.

My illness continued for a couple of weeks, I think, until one afternoon I woke up and found myself in Banpotphisai 'cottage' hospital. I was in a private room and Seckson was asleep under the bed. He had been living in the hospital for many days, taking care of me while I was treated for 'food poisoning'. He was actually my nurse, for Thai country hospitals are frequently very short-staffed and it is often left to the family not only to feed the patient but also to change their bedding and even to see to their various 'drips', of which I seemed to have plenty.

The only resident doctor at the tiny hospital was very nice and very young, just out of medical school, and I think he was a little bit nervous of treating such a rarity as a Phra Farang, as though my internal organs might be different from other people's. After a few days, he decided I didn't have food poisoning at all and started treating me for bronchitis. Happily, a few weeks later, by which time I was in the province's main hospital in Nakhon Sawan city, my pneumonia had largely cleared up.

I was staying on the top floor of the hospital in a ward reserved for monks. On the first day that I felt strong enough to get out of bed, I took a short stroll around the ward and some of the corridors. From one of the windows, I could see the top of a huge old brick chedi, together with the multi-tiered roof of a very grand-looking Bote. On the top of a tree-covered mountainous hill behind the monastery gleamed a gigantic golden Buddha image, staring out across the country. The impressive effect was somewhat diminished by five very tall red and white transmitting aerials nearby. I asked a nurse the name of the monastery. "Wat Khao Kob", she said.

I knew immediately that the Monastery of Frog Mountain would be my next home.

Why should I want to move from my pleasant and quiet environment at Wat Nahoob to what was obviously a big, important temple in the middle of a noisy city? Partly at least because of a passing comment Dav had made in the gardens of Wat Buddhapadipa. He had said that after a couple of years as a monk in Thailand, I might find myself becoming "complacent." I made no reply, but his words set off alarm bells in my mind. Complacent. The word is actually anathema to me and throughout my life, in whatever situation, environment or relationship I had found myself in, I had always been careful to watch out for this state of unreasonable self-satisfaction.

Lying in my hospital bed, I had taken the opportunity to look objectively at my life at Wat Nahoob and I realised I was becoming complacent. I was also sabbai, but that was quite a different thing.

At Wat Nahoob I had everything I needed: a delightful little kuti in a beautiful forest setting; I admired and respected my abbot; I got on well with the village people; I had all the food and time I needed; I was slowly beginning to learn some of the more important chanting and I had cleared away my doubts. All these things were what created my sabbai. The complacency was really the other side of the same coin; the darker side of sabbai, and for me it was a definite danger, a potential hindrance, for it could lead to torpor and apathy. A monk should always be satisfied with things and situations just as they are but not (in my opinion) to the point where his mind becomes stagnant.

I liked Nahoob and everything and everybody connected with my life there, but I felt no 'clinging' or attachment for it and was quite prepared to move if by doing so, I could make progress, or stop myself regressing.

Even before I saw the roof of Wat Kob's Uposatha Hall, I knew it would soon be time to leave Wat Nahoob, but I had no idea at all about where I would go. Back to Bangkok? No, my physical health wasn't really good enough to subject it to the capital's fumes. A big monastery or another small one? Country or city? It didn't matter, as long as I shattered my complacency. The Frog Temple would do as well as any other.

As things turned out, it did very well indeed.

* The Students' Education Trust. At present, the trust supports 19 students at university or in other higher education establishments and is itself now supported by companies and other charitable trusts in the UK.

Chapter 23

Wat Kob's official and 'modern' name is Wat Worranatbanpot, but most people know it by its original name. For more than 700 years, the monastery has been a place of pilgrimage for those willing to climb the 437 steps leading to the hill top to pay their respects to the ancient images and 'footprint' of the Buddha that are kept there. Since 1991, Wat Kob has been a Royal Temple, one of more than a hundred that are supported by HM the King.

In fact, the main part of the monastery is now at the base of Khao Kob and the upper part is occupied by only a handful of monks who wish to be isolated from the busy city far below. During the Rains Retreat there may be more than 50 monks and novices living in the bottom part of the monastery.

Wat Kob is big, covering an area of more than 43 acres and it seems it has always been an important temple. Two engraved stones* have been found at the monastery, one of which records how Phraya Thammikkarat and a group of Thai monks brought two Buddha 'footprints'** from Ceylon in about 1220, a gift from the government of that country in gratitude for Thailand's help in re-establishing Buddhism there. The right footprint is at Wat Trapang Thong in Sukhothai and the stone records that the left was placed on the mountain top of 'Pak Phra Bang' which is the old name for Nakhon Sawan.

The other stone records that Wat Kob was originally built by Phraya Ban Muang, a ruler of the kingdom of Sukhothai, in memory of his brother who died on the mountain. When he established Wat Kob, he built chedis, viharns and Buddha images and the monastery was surrounded by a lotus-filled moat, bamboo groves and Bo trees. The bamboo groves and moat are long gone, but some of the ancient buildings and relics remain.

The chedi that I had seen from the hospital window is from the Sukhothai period and contains the relics of the brother of Phraya Ban Muang. The chedi is about 32 metres high and was originally covered in plaster. That has almost all fallen off now, revealing the dull red bricks of the chedi's construction. The chedi actually looks as if it is in imminent danger of falling over, for it seems to have twisted about half way up and leans at a definite angle. In an ancient viharn nearby is a magnificent 38-foot-long reclining Buddha image from the Sukhothai period made, I have been told, from a single piece of teak covered in plaster and gold leaf.

The monastery's huge, new Uposatha Hall dwarfs a nearly 600-year-old tiny Bote that stands nearby. In the old Bote is a frieze of delightful mural paintings showing scenes from the Buddha's life. They are painted in a particularly naive style as though they were the work of a child. This Bote is not the original Uposatha of Wat Kob, for in another area are much older stone arches that mark the 'Sima' or consecrated ground of an earlier Bote.

Despite the monastery's obvious importance, very little is known of its early history and it was deserted for many centuries, though nobody knows why. Its buildings and images, then already centuries old, became ruins overgrown by shrubs and trees—until Luang Por Tong arrived .

Luang Por Tong must have been an extraordinary monk. He was born in Utaradit, north of Nakhon Sawan, in 1856 and became a monk when he was 21. In 1882 when he was wandering around the country he visited the ruins of Wat Kob. The people of the city asked him to stay there for the three-month Rains Retreat. He stayed for 59 years until he died in 1941, aged 85. Luang Por Tong made it his life's work to begin the restoration of Wat Kob and it is largely due to him that the ancient buildings are in such good condition.

Legends have grown up around Luang Por Tong's name and even when he was alive many people believed he had acquired supernatural powers. He was a very strict and devout monk: always wearing robes taken from a coffin just before the funeral pyre was lit; always living at the base of a tree and never failing to go out on binderbaht. Even when he could no longer walk, he had a tricycle on which he would go out on his alms round.

There is a story that he was on a scaffold repairing the very top of the old chedi, when he fell 30 metres to the ground. He was completely unharmed and immediately climbed back up the scaffold. Another story relates how he could miraculously 'shorten distances'. He was seen on binderbaht in villages many miles from Wat Kob though it was quite impossible for him to have got to the villages by any 'normal' manner.

Yet another story says that he could not be photographed. The film always came out blank. There is only one known photograph of him, for which he gave permission, and that is today on the abbot's sermon seat.

Just outside the monastery's boundary wall, on what was presumably once temple property, is a very large and deep pond full of enormous old turtles and huge fish. There is a story that Luang Por Tong actually dug this pond himself, using his alms-bowl to carry the earth away.

Luang Por Tong left another small mystery, two in fact, named Ta Kob and Yai Khiat. They are the life-sized stone figures of a grandfather (Ta Kob) and grandmother (Yai Khiat). They are really very strange indeed and they sit in recently-built little shelters in front of the old Bote. People leave gifts of tobacco and betel nuts for them and in recent times, someone has given grandfather a pair of plastic spectacles (and more recently, a gold Batman mask!) but there is no record to show who the figures actually represented or why Luang Por Tong had them made.

Even today, many local people attribute supernatural power to anything associated with Luang Por Tong. In the new Bote is a display case with Luang Por Tong brass and bronze images for sale, as well as amulets to be worn around the neck. These amulets, some claim, can protect the devout wearer from bullets. Before anybody laughs that story off, there is a series of a dozen photographs in the Bote taken in 1994 which show the arrest of a gunman who shot a rival in Nakhon Sawan city. Others in the series show a doctor removing several bullets from the victim's chest. The victim is smiling and proudly showing his Luang Por Tong amulet, bent by the assailant's bullets, and he appears to have been only superficially injured.........

The ashes of Luang Por Tong are now enshrined in the Bote, with a painting of the old monk. In the monastery grounds is a shrine with a life-sized image of Luang Por Tong and many people go there daily to pay their respects.

Luang Por Tong is the first recorded abbot of Wat Kob. The second was Phra Khru Thammakhun (abbot from 1942-1963) but it is with the third and present abbot that the modern history of Wat Worranatbanpot begins. As Luang Por Tong saved Wat Kob from total ruin, so Phra Suthee Thammasopon has not only carried on his predecessor's work, but built upon it, to make the monastery the important religious centre it is today.

When Luang Por Suthee became abbot in 1964, he saw in the spacious grounds the opportunity to create a modern, working monastery, retaining the traditions of the past but with all the facilities that a 20th century monastery needs. His vision included a full-sized school for monks where they could study Dhamma, the Vinaya and the Pali language; modern accommodation, simple and functional, befitting the monks' lifestyle, but clean and easy to maintain; a new sala to accommodate thousands of people and a new Bote, big enough for the large number of monks and novices who would eventually live at the monastery. With the willing support of the laypeople he has achieved it all, and more.

The new Uposatha Hall, completed in 1990 at a cost of nine million Baht, has something of the grandness of a cathedral. It is certainly one of the tallest Botes I have seen, though its outside dimensions are misleading. Half the height of the building is actually 'attic' and inside it seems considerably, smaller than from the outside. The outside decoration has all the ornateness of most Thai temples but, again, this is misleading, for inside it is simpler than most. A grey marble floor, much of it raised about eight inches to make a higher level for the monks than for the novices or laypeople, and cream-painted walls without murals. The main Buddha image is large and modern and the alter decorations are simple and subdued. There are lots of candles and flowers but, unlike many Thai Botes, it is not cluttered with all sorts of strange 'religious' artifacts.

The present abbot has also been responsible for the building of the monastery's crematorium, one of the few I have seen with a double oven. Funerals are an important source of revenue for any monastery in Thailand and one the size of Wat Kob needs a huge income just for its maintenance and upkeep.

Luang Por Suthee also has his own ideas about the environment.

Unfortunately many monasteries in Thailand are simply not clean or tidy and he was determined that his monastery would not be the same. And it isn't. I have visited many hundreds of monasteries in Thailand, in cities, towns and villages, and Wat Kob is undoubtedly one of the cleanest and neatest of them all. It even has its own skip for rubbish, the only one I have seen outside of Bangkok, and it is changed every week.

Luang Por Suthee has carried on Luang Por Tong's work by having the old Bote renovated. The viharn, containing the reclining Buddha, has been rebuilt to give better protection for the ancient image and he has also established a walled meditation garden, thick with mango trees and a few small kutis for monks who want to meditate undisturbed.

I didn't know any of this as I stood staring out of the hospital window. I only knew that I wanted to live there, but doing that wouldn't be a certainty until I had paid my respects to the abbot and had asked his permission. A visit was in order.

One of my students from Nahoob, Mit Sridet, studied at a school in the city and during the week, stayed at a friend's house close to the school. The house was in a lane that ran along one side of the monastery.

Mit's English is almost fluent and after I was discharged from the hospital, I asked him to accompany me on a visit to Wat Kob to act as interpreter in case the abbot couldn't speak English. Mit told me that the monastery was sometimes known locally as 'the frog that eats people', on account of the number of cremations that were held there.

We walked into Wat Kob and by chance met the abbot almost immediately. I made a respectful wai but before Mit or I could say anything the abbot asked, "Are you better now?" "Yes, thank you", I replied, wondering how on earth he had known I had been ill.

I didn't know at the time that the abbot is a very high-ranking monk, with the title Chao Khun***, and he is responsible for a number of monasteries in the province, including Wat Nahoob. (Since then, he has been appointed religious governer of Nakhon Sawan with the responsibility for all the province's monasteries.) It transpired that he already knew a great deal about me indeed and that Acharn Waow had once been the abbot's looksit, or attendant, when they both lived at Wat Somciel in Banphotpisai. I asked the abbot if he would allow me to wander around the monastery for a while and he gave his permission. I gave another wai and said goodbye.

Mit and I had only been walking around for a few minutes when a monk approached us and, speaking in English, invited us to his room for a chat. Phra Maha Sutont had been a monk for about 20 years so he was quite senior and his English was very good but, well, a bit odd sometimes. He had cleverly taught himself by listening to the radio and from a couple of very old books of idioms, one English and one American. He would occasionally call me 'my dear fellow' or exclaim 'shucks!', sometimes in the same sentence, but we got on extremely well and on that very first meeting he suggested I should consider living at Wat Kob. We could be 'buddies', he said.

During the next few weeks, I made several visits to the monastery and on a couple of occasions stayed overnight in a room next to Phra Maha Sutont's, in one of the new kuti blocks. These two-storey buildings are like modern apartment blocks and each of the four buildings contains 16 single rooms, as well as communal toilets and showers. The rooms are excellent and each has parquet flooring, mosquito screens at the windows and security grills which are unfortunately very necessary in Thailand, even in monasteries.

It was about a month before the beginning of the Pansa and many of the new rainy season monks had already ordained and were living in the blocks, together with their stereos, TVs and radios. I obviously had no objections to that but I thought the noise level at night was sometimes inappropriate for a monastic environment. In fact, it was horrendous! I knew I would not be happy to stay there long-term but I had already made up my mind that I would live at the monastery. I asked Phra Maha Sutont if we could request the abbot's permission.

After a few minutes deliberation, the abbot said I was welcome and that I could live in one of the new kuti blocks, or in the mango garden, or chose some other empty kuti in the monastery grounds. In fact, I had already decided on the kuti I wanted. At the back of the monastery and fairly isolated from the main areas were three large, old, wooden kutis on stilts, all very ramshackle and in need of repair. Two of them were occupied but the middle of the three had been empty for some years. Despite the fact that it was falling to bits, it looked charming and would, I thought, be quieter than the new rooms. The abbot and Phra Maha Sutont tried to dissuade me from the idea because many of the temple boys lived in tiny rooms under the kutis and, said the abbot, they were very noisy indeed. I doubted that they could be noisier than some of the new monks, but didn't say so. My mind was made up, the old kuti would be my new home.

* Now in the National Museum, Bangkok.

** Buddha 'footprint': the Buddha is believed to have had curious designs or whorls on the soles of his feet. Natural rock formations, sometimes of huge size, are occasionally found which resemble these designs. Alternatively, 'footprints' may be cast in concrete and covered in gold leaf.

*** Chao Khun, pronounced Chao Koon: a monastic title which has been translated as 'Lord Abbot' but also as 'His Excellency'.

Chapter 24

The ramshackle wooden kuti is still my home, though it is now in considerably better shape than it was. After I first moved in I had a lot of work to do just to get the place habitable and the abbot left me to settle in for a couple of weeks before he paid his first visit, accompanied by Phra Maha Sutont to translate.

It had already become very obvious to me that Maha Sutont was extremely nervous of being in the abbot's company. He almost seemed to be frightened of the abbot. Whenever the three of us needed to meet, he would be sweating and visibly trembling, though I couldn't see why at all. To me the abbot seemed to be quite a jolly fellow. I described him to a friend in England as being a bit like Father Christmas; without the hair and beard, of course.

I wasn't at all sure then how I should relate to the abbot. We were at extreme and opposite ends of the Sangha hierarchy. I was a new and very junior monk and he was very senior and held high religious office. It's not a criticism of Thai people to say that I believe they are quite impressed by titles, uniforms and social status. I am not particularly impressed by them. I had met many very senior monks and had always gladly shown the correct level of respect for them, triple bows and all that, as befitted our relative stations, but these were only outward forms. I didn't know them. Before I ordained I had learned a hard lesson from a senior monk that I had deeply respected. At the time, he had seemed the epitome of what a Buddhist monk should be. He fooled me (and millions of Thai people too); he turned out to be a liar, a cheat and a womaniser and was forced to disrobe. I won't make that mistake again. I have no more pedestals.

The abbot and Maha Sutont came to my kuti and the abbot lowered himself into a chair. We sat on the floor. The abbot regarded me silently but benevolently for a time and then said: "You're very thin". This is true. I looked pointedly at his rotund belly and replied: "And you, Venerable Sir, are very fat", equally truthfully. Maha Sutont began to quiver nervously. "I'm not fat", said the abbot and pulled up his ungsa to reveal a very round belly hanging over the top of his sabong. "Yes, you are", I said and poked his belly with my finger, causing both it and Maha Sutont to shake violently. I'm sure Maha Sutont wasn't used to hearing the abbot spoken to in this way and he looked about ready to fling himself off my balcony, but the abbot roared with laughter; I believe he might have found it quite refreshing to be spoken to plainly. From that moment our relationship seemed to be established. He frequently tells people that I am not a 'normal' monk, though quite what he means by that, I'm not sure!

Since that first meeting, I have gradually developed a very great deal of respect for the abbot and make a point of showing it with a triple bow whenever the opportunity arises. I enjoy it because I think he genuinely deserves respect, not because he is the abbot and my 'boss', nor because he is a Chao Khun, but because of what I believe he really is inside, underneath the titles and the robe. I don't place him on a pedestal and I don't 'worship' him, but I like him enormously. He's not always jolly and although I have never seen him angry or heard him raise his voice, I have seen him turn wayward novices to stone merely with a look.

Sometimes when we are walking on binderbaht, or even chanting in the Bote, he will glance at me and smile, sometimes he even bursts out laughing. I'm not sure what the joke is (me, perhaps) but I always respond in kind and whenever I see him, I want to smile and perhaps poke him in the belly.

Smiling is about the only type of communication that we have, unless I call in an interpreter-student, though we both try. The abbot once, quite inexplicably, said 'hot water' to me, but that is the only time I have ever heard him speak English. On the rare occasions when I need to ask or tell him something, I carefully look up the required vocabulary in my English-Thai dictionary and write out what I want to say, paying particular attention to the tones.

It is the Thai tones that prevent many foreigners from ever speaking the language well. There are five tones and every word needs to be pronounced in the correct one, otherwise a completely different word to the one intended may be used. Some words which are phonetically the same may have four or five quite different meanings when used with different tones. The words for 'near' and 'far', for example, are phonetically the same—both klay—but one is spoken with a low tone and one with a falling tone. I have suffered with tinnitus for many years and have great difficulty sometimes hearing any tones at all. I invariably pronounce my words in entirely the wrong tone and frequently come out with the most bizarre and sometimes embarrassing statements. I once quite innocently asked a rather grand Thai lady if she had ever eaten penis! On another occasion I told Acharn Waow that I was going to Banphot town. When he asked me how I would get there I told him I would walk, "with one foot up my bottom".

The best opportunity to speak to the abbot is directly after evening chanting. I start to approach him, my carefully rehearsed lines running through my head. A look of panic appears on his face and his eyes dart from side to side, seeking an escape from what he knows is going to be a mystical and mystifying experience. The novices who have started to get up from their places at the back of the Bote immediately sit down again, with excited and expectant whispers of "the Phra Farang's going to speak Thai", and giggles sweep over them.

I approach the abbot and, my hands held in a respectful wai, state my piece: "The roof of my kuti has a leak". He looks at me for a moment, seeking some sense in whatever it was I actually said, and then says something like, "Have you been to the doctor?" I frequently misunderstand what he said too, so my reply to his question might well, and usually does, add to the absolute gibberish.

I once told him I wanted a plastic mat for my kuti and he asked me in amazement what I was going to do with it. I said I wanted to sit on it of course. He told me the monastery storeroom didn't have any as far as he knew and I replied that I had seen hundreds of them, all over the place. He simply looked at me very strangely and sympathetically before hurrying back to his kuti for a lie-down. Unfortunately I had told him I wanted a plastic tiger to sit on.

We can go on like this for several minutes, our conversations doing justice to a book of Zen koans, until finally one of us gives up. He usually gives a non-committal grunt, I respectfully wai, the roof of my kuti continues to leak and I don't have a mat. As I walk out of the Bote the novices stare at me in awe.

Although I never had communication problems with Phra Maha Sutont, our relationship never did develop into becoming 'buddies'. His behaviour over the first few months that I lived at Wat Kob started to become very erratic indeed, though he was always pleasant to me. His behaviour became more and more weird and one day he simply wasn't there anymore. I never really knew why, or where he had gone. He had simply moved on.

There were some moments in my first few months at Wat Kob when I thought perhaps I should move on too, but when I examined those thoughts objectively, I realised that Wat Kob really is as good as anywhere else, so I have stayed.

At those times, I remember a story about the late Phra Acharn Chaa, the much-revered teacher of many Phra Farang at his international forest monastery, Wat Pah Nanachat, in Thailand's northeast. Acharn Chaa was talking about a monk who was always going from one monastery to another, looking for the 'ideal' environment. Acharn Chaa likened him to a man "with shit on his sandals, always looking for a place that didn't smell and not realising that he carried the smell with him". In another version I have heard, he told his monks to watch the monastery dogs and notice how they would sit down in a place, scratch, move to another place, scratch and move again, always scratching and moving and looking for a place that didn't have fleas; not knowing that they carried the fleas with them wherever they went.*

My 'fleas' were never too bothersome but they occasionally caused me to stop and try to think objectively about my life at Wat Kob, and even sometimes my life as a monk.

Binderbaht at Wat Kob gave me food for thought as well as food for my belly for a while and I started each day feeling guilty and greedy. On my first day of living at the monastery, the abbot invited me to go out on binderbaht with him each morning. He never misses binderbaht and usually about six monks accompany him, together with their looksits.

Our route is a fairly long one and takes about an hour, going through residential, commercial and market areas. The people in Nakhon Sawan are extremely generous and many offer food. Each person puts a couple of spoonfuls of rice in our bowls and then adds a plastic bag of curry, dessert and so on. As soon as the food is put into the monk's bowl, his looksit immediately takes it out and transfers it to a carrier bag, leaving just the plain rice in the bowl.

Halfway through the route we are met by a motorcycle onto which the looksits load the carrier bags, by then very full, and collect new empty bags for the second part of the route. By the time we finish binderbaht and return to the monastery, these bags are also full. Meanwhile each monk's first bag has been delivered to his room or kuti. Everyday, I finish my binderbaht round with four and sometimes five carrier bags full of food, plus about eight lbs of rice.

From all that food, I take only a very little for my breakfast and a little more is put aside for my lunch, perhaps just an apple or other fruit. The rest I give to my looksit and another temple boy living beneath my kuti. I only feed two boys, because although there are a dozen or more living under the three kutis, most of them are attached as looksit to a particular monk and usually get their daily food from that monk. Even after my two boys have taken all the food they need for the day, there are still three or four carrier bags full, plus a considerable quantity of rice. This is all thrown away. Everyday.

When that much food is multiplied by the number of monks and novices who go out on binderbaht, it must add up to a very great deal of food wasted daily, (though not every monk walks on binderbaht over such a long route or for such a long time).

Besides being a useless waste, the food is frequently offered by poor people and they may give the monks better food than they themselves eat. Additionally, the food is given in good faith and, I thought at first, the people presumably expect the monks to eat it. Or had going out on binderbaht become merely a symbolic gesture concerned more with 'making merit' than actually feeding the monks?

I was not at all happy about this situation for a while. For some years before ordaining, I had worked voluntarily for a UK charity** which raises money to help poor children in Thailand's northeastern region. Many of these children are malnourished, or at least undernourished. Although it was an illogical sentiment, I felt guilty that I wasted more food everyday than many of them ate in a month.

I turned to the Vinaya or, more specifically, to the definitive commentary on the Vinaya rules, written by the late 10th Supreme Patriarch, in which he explains every rule in a modern context. The late Supreme Patriarch wrote: "A bhikku is prohibited from accepting almsfood above (the top edge of his bowl) because to accept more would be to show greed. According to the traditions of the present day, to accept much on the basis of greediness is censurable, while to accept much on the basis of Metta (loving-kindness) is not censurable".

If a monk personally feels he is collecting too much food, the answer would appear to be simple, not to go out on binderbaht for so long or so far. But if the monk only walks on binderbaht close to his monastery, people who live some distance away may be deprived of the opportunity to offer food. It can take only a few minutes for the bowl to be filled, but if a monk walks for such a short time, is he really getting any spiritual benefit from the experience, or is he merely 'shopping' for his breakfast?

Despite the late Supreme Patriarch's commentary, my 'social conscience' was still pricked each day. Eventually I put some of my questions about binderbaht to a few teacher-students who visited me one day. I asked at what point should relatively modern traditions be allowed to compromise the monks' life-style, and whether the culture should outweigh the monks' rules as laid down from the earliest times of Buddhism.

Somewhat to my surprise, there was general agreement amongst the students that the monk *should* accept as much food as the people wanted to offer, even though most of it would be thrown away. The students said that the donors were usually fully aware that the monk couldn't possibly eat all the food but that the point was in the giving, not in the receiving. They agreed that the monk should show Metta and allow the people to'make merit.' OK. My questions were answered and I continued to go out on binderbaht with the abbot—according to the traditions of the present day.

Another small incident made me think quite hard for a time. When I had first moved to the monastery, I decided I would start teaching English again though not to the same extent that I had been doing at Nahoob. Wat Kob is only a short walk or bus ride from all the important schools in the province, including the teacher training, technical and vocational colleges. I had taught or lectured at most of them on an ad hoc basis but as they were more than an hour's bus ride from Nahoob, it had never been very convenient.

Some of the teachers from the vocational college visited me at Wat Kob and asked if I would teach a communication skills course, to which I readily agreed, though I explained that I would not allow teaching to interfere with my meditation or other studies. I suggested they draw up a time-table, which they did, and when we had all agreed on the shape and content of the course, I rather belatedly suggested that they should formally ask the abbot for his permission. They went to see him and the abbot said 'No'.

I couldn't believe it and went with Mit to see him one evening, determined to change his mind. Why, I asked, would he not allow me to teach? I explained that the students would benefit from being taught by a native speaker and I very much wanted to teach so that I could return something to the Thai people for their many kindnesses to me. But he was adamant. He explained that a monk should be above the world and the problems of the laity, whilst remaining compassionate for them.

The abbot went on to explain that if I was teaching Dhamma that would be acceptable, but to teach English was too much like a 'job', regardless of whether I was being paid for it or not, and the monk should not 'work' for the laity. This seemed to be the exact opposite of Acharn Waow's view, for he had not only actively encouraged me to teach at the local high school but had also offered my services to other schools in the district. (I have never, incidentally, accepted money for teaching.)

I thought about his words for a long time, even wondering briefly if perhaps I had made a mistake in coming to live at Wat Kob with such an unreasonable abbot. I finally told the teachers to tear up the schedule. I think if the abbot had left it to me to make my own decision after his little lecture, I probably would have taught, though I would never have been sure if that was the right decision.

As is often the case, things turned out quite well in the end. The abbot certainly had no objection to people coming to see me at my kuti and I began teaching, or really just having conversations, with teachers, some of whom had never had the opportunity to talk with a native speaker before. In a way this was more productive and far-reaching than actually teaching the students.

Although it is not a question that plays on my mind or raises any doubts, I do sometimes wonder how far the monks' social responsibility should go in the 20th century. Theoretically, I think we have none at all and yet, using education as an example, prior to about 1930, before the government started building new schools, nearly all schools in Thailand were in monasteries and the teachers were mostly monks, teaching all subjects, not just Dhamma.***

Some monks obviously do feel they have social responsibilities. I have visited a very isolated monastery in another province where the abbot has turned his monastery into an AIDS hospice. I believe it is the first such hospice in Thailand. He has many hundreds of patients, some of whom live at the monastery and others who go for daily treatment. He has also raised funds to build a 16-bed hospital at the monastery for those in the final stages of the disease. He now receives help from the government and both praise and condemnation from other monks. I was immensely impressed by what he is doing, but I could not honestly say if it is right or wrong of him to be doing it as a monk.

* My apologies to the monks of Wat Pah Nanachat if I have related these stories incorrectly.

** The Anglo-Thai Foundation.

*** In 1931, 87% of schools in Nakhon Sawan Province were in monasteries.

Chapter 25

Towards the end of each year, I start looking at the calendar in an increasingly dejected mood. It's visa renewal time again and that usually means hassle.

Once you know the procedure it's actually quite straightforward, but still involves a lot of to-ing and fro-ing to various official departments in Bangkok with all the associated nightmare that travelling anywhere in Bangkok brings. It's actually more difficult and complicated for a monk to renew his visa than it is for an 'ordinary' applicant, though there are good reasons for this.

I believe for visitors to Thailand who simply want to extend their holiday by a few more weeks the procedure is relatively simple. Go to the Immigration Department visa office, fill in a form, pay the fee and get the passport stamped. Other foreigners who need an extension for three months, or six months, depending on their reasons, face more difficulties and waiting time but the process is still relatively straightforward (though judging by the number of frustrated-looking foreigners I have seen at the visa office, there might be many who would disagree).

Foreign monks are entitled to a twelve-month visa, though it is by no means automatic. The first time I needed to apply, I thought the monks' high status in Thailand would make the procedure fairly painless and free of difficulties, but at the visa office everybody is just a foreigner and all are treated equally, regardless of what they are wearing or their social status. I'm sure that the Immigration Department officials don't deliberately put up any barriers to make life awkward for Western Buddhist monks, but they seem to be a bit more cautious before banging away with their innumerable rubber stamps and handing out the very desirable twelve-month extensions. That caution is justified for it certainly isn't unknown for young foreign men, at the end of not only their visas but also their money, to suddenly 'get religion' and try to ordain as monks.

I had encounters with such people myself when I stayed at Wat Mahadhatu. Occasionally, I would be called to the Section 5 reception desk to meet and talk with young Western men who claimed they wanted to attend a residential meditation course or even that they wanted to ordain as monks. Often these Westerners were quite genuine and we tried to help them as much as we could, but just as often, they were very obviously not. The crunch always came when they were told that before going any further that we would need to see their passports to check their status within Thailand. Usually their visas had already expired, or were about to do so.

I heard that after I moved from Bangkok to Nakhon Sawan there was such a case when a young European was accepted for ordination. In fact, he was ordained by the abbot of Wat Mahadhatu, I believe only the second Westerner to have had that honour. He was given help in applying for a twelve-month visa so that he could continue his 'Dhamma and meditation studies' and then as soon as he had it, he simply walked out of Section 5 wearing the jeans and tee-shirt he had arrived in, leaving his robes in a pile on the floor of his room. The Section 5 monk who told me this story said that the abbot was far from happy—I don't doubt it—and that the monastery would in future be far more cautious in its dealings with Westerners.

I had originally arrived in Thailand with a three-month visa which was due to expire a couple of months after I had ordained. Phra Maha Laow and Acharn Amara Thera had both returned to England by then and I had nobody to help or advise me. I knew the first step was to go to the Religious Affairs Department, which is part of the Ministry of Education, and get a special form for Western monks. This form asks 40 questions, helpfully written only in Thai and I had to find a translator to help me complete it. Once completed, the form had to be signed three times; by my Upachaya, by the religious governor of Bangkok district and by the religious governor of the province. In my case my Upachaya and the religious governor of the province were one and the same and I made an appointment to see the abbot of Wat Mahadhatu to request his two signatures.

I had to wait a couple of days for an appointment. There was no problem about the abbot signing the form as my Upachaya but he said he couldn't sign as the provincial governor until the district governor had already signed. Fair enough, so I made an appointment with the district governor, the abbot of Bangkok's Wat Po, waited a couple of days until he was available and got the form signed. Then back to my Upachaya, another day or so of waiting, and he signed for the second time.

I returned to the Religious Affairs Department and handed over the form and a photocopy of my passport. "Where's your letter?", asked the official. "What letter?", I replied. "The letter from your Upachaya to say why you want to extend your visa". In fact this is exactly the information that is already on the form which was signed by my Upachaya. Never mind, back to my Upachaya who by then had gone away on official business to another province for a few days. On his return, he had his secretary-monk prepare the necessary letter which I then delivered to the Religious Affairs Department. They told me to return in seven days for a letter from them to the Immigration Department requesting the twelve-month visa.

I waited a week and returned as instructed. My file had been lost and I was told to come back the following week. I was becoming a little concerned because by this time my old visa had expired and I was theoretically an illegal alien. I naively hoped that my status as a monk would make that unimportant but when I eventually arrived at the visa office, clutching my various bits of paperwork, it was politely pointed out to me that before any progress on the new visa could be made I would have to pay 2,000 Baht for my overstay, as well as 500 Baht in advance for the new stamp.

I had only recently become a monk and there was still very much more Mr Peter Robinson in me than there was Phra Peter Pannapadipo. I found myself in both a potentially confrontational situation and an embarrassing one, since I didn't have 2,000 Baht. I really try to avoid confrontations as much as I can, but I could feel my European hackles rising at what seemed to be the injustice of the situation. This is conditioned response, of course.

I was about to point out in no uncertain terms to the young officer (who was actually very nice and very professionally polite) that (1) I was a monk and that therefore (2) the Vinaya rules prevented me from dealing with money or buying and selling, (3) that it was the inefficiency of another Thai government department that had caused me to overstay and that (4) as far as I was concerned such mundane and worldly matters as visas and passports were of no importance whatsoever. All this I'm sure would justifiably have fallen on deaf ears and it only goes to show how pompous and naive I was at that time.

I was just getting my righteous indignation nicely worked up when happily the potential and no doubt one-sided confrontation was avoided when another officer walked into the room. We recognised each other immediately. We had met very briefly on a railway station some years before when Phra Maha Laow and I were about to board an overnight train for a visit to Sisaket province in the northeast. The officer, Khun Tanacom, had been Phra Maha Laow's looksit many years ago.

I presume he was senior to the officer I was about to lamblast for he took me aside, looked through all my papers and asked me to wait. He left the office but within ten minutes returned to say that the head of the visa section had not only waived my overstay fine but had actually paid my 500 Baht visa fee himself. Added to that, he had given me 100 Baht for my taxi fare back to Wat Mahadhatu.

I felt immensely grateful and extremely humbled. Even though I had not actually confronted the young officer with an indignant, ridiculous and typically Western outburst, I was embarrassed that I had even considered it.

After that my dealings with the visa office on that application went very smoothly. I was issued a temporary visa and told to return the following month, by which time my application would have been considered and either rejected or approved. The following month I collected my twelve-month visa.

Unfortunately for me, Phra Maha Laow's ex-looksit moved to some other department soon after, so in following years I had to manage on my own. However, I know the routine now and since that first year, it has become progressively easier, especially since the officer who always deals with my case, Khun Vinnai, now knows my passport with its masses of visas and extensions very well. There's still a lot of to-ing and fro-ing, especially now that I live in a monastery that is more than five hours bus and taxi ride away from the offices I need to visit, but my dealings with the officers are always cordial and good-tempered.

Unfortunately, when making my application a couple of years ago, I discovered that not only my visa but also my passport was about to expire. This necessitated a nightmare of journeying between Nakhon Sawan and Bangkok, the British Consulate, the Religious Affairs Department and the Immigration Department, as well as the abbots from whom I needed signatures. You can't get a visa without a valid passport and you can't get a passport without a valid visa. A 'Catch 22' situation only resolved by a very helpful Thai lady at the British Embassy.

Whilst at the visa office, I have met, or at least observed, many other Westerners applying for visas of various durations. I have occasionally been absolutely appalled by their behaviour and very much admire the Thai officers' 'cool' and almost continual politeness in dealing with some of these wretched people. Some seem to have made no effort whatsoever to understand what constitutes polite or impolite behaviour in Thai society. In their manner of speaking, acting and even dressing, they constantly insult their hosts, not deliberately, I'm sure, but simply out of ignorance of Thai ways.

I notice this in the street as well. Because we rarely see farang in Nakhon Sawan, all my time is spent with Thai people and I am sure I have gradually and unconsciously changed to adopt many Thai norms of behaviour (as well as monk norms of behaviour). When I have occasion to visit Bangkok, I quickly realise that I now see Westerners, at least partly, in the way the Thai people must see them and I am frequently embarrassed by what I see.

Once when I was staying at Wat Mahadhatu, I was asked by an angry group of Thai people to ask a Western couple to leave the monastery. The couple, a young man and woman in their twenties, were sitting on the floor of the Bote, wearing the skimpiest shorts I have ever seen, with their legs stretched out and their feet pointed at the main Buddha image. I politely explained the basic rules of conduct when visiting a Thai monastery and was told in no uncertain terms to... well, to go away. But at least they left the Bote soon after. I was extremely embarrassed and apologised to the Thai laypeople, but happily the incident, once over, fell into the 'mai bpen rai' category.

Perhaps that was rather an extreme case, but I often see examples of less obviously bad behaviour which I know causes offence to many Thais, particularly those who have less contact with Westerners. It is, of course, easier to be judgemental about the behaviour of others than it is about one's own behaviour. Perhaps I also still make many stupid errors, but I am sure the Buddha's teaching about mindfulness, about being aware of one's actions or speech from moment to moment, has helped me a lot in this respect. But sometimes I can't help wondering if some of the Westerners who visit Thailand have even taken the trouble to read a guide-book to the country. The books invariably explain the most basic social 'dos and don'ts', but frequently the attitude amongst some Westerners seems to be the wrong side of 'mai bpen rai': a sort of "I'll do whatever I want to do and it doesn't matter" attitude, which is very sad.

One silly mistake I made was to cause intense embarrassment to a Thai man and regrettably he was another monk. After Phra Maha

Sutont left Wat Kob there was only one monk remaining who could speak any English. Phra Suthee was a young man who had been a monk for about five years at the time. He is very small and looks much younger than his 26 years, in fact he looks like a schoolboy and has a sense of humour to match. We get on extremely well though occasionally come to verbal blows when we discuss our differing views of what constitutes 'real' Buddhism.

I had once conducted a survey amongst my school students in which I asked them what their hobbies were. To my surprise at the top of the list was 'sleeping', followed by 'visiting Fairyland'. Fairyland is a department store in the centre of Nakhon Sawan city. I was interested to visit this emporium to find out what the great attraction was for my students, as it seemed a very odd hobby. I asked Phra Suthee if he would like to accompany me.

He was horrified at the idea of a monk going into a department store, which quite mystified me. He explained that it was acceptable for a monk to go to an 'ordinary' little shop if he needed to buy something, but a monk shouldn't go to a 'big' shop. This was somewhat lacking in logic to me (Western logic, that is) because I had grown up in a country where department stores were on virtually every high street and were simply considered convenient places to shop. (I didn't like to tell my friend that whilst living in London, I had frequently escorted Thai monks from Wat Buddhapadipa around such 'shops' as Harrods etc., which they seemed to love visiting, even though they rarely bought anything).

I could see that despite Phra Suthee's objections he was actually quite excited by my rather naughty idea, and he eventually agreed to go with me. Having about 20 Baht between us, we weren't intending to actually do any shopping but nevertheless set off with a feeling of going on a great adventure.

Fairyland is modelled along Western store lines, with cosmetics on the ground floor, clothes on the second, electrical goods on the third and so on. We walked through the main doors and I with my huge strides was halfway through the first department before I became aware of where we were. Phra Suthee, hurrying to keep up with me, suddenly stopped dead in his tracks. I have never actually seen a Thai person's face turn bright red before but my friend's face did just that. "Oh..oh...oh", he said in a little strangled voice as he found himself completely surrounded by displays of plastic female torsos wearing only knickers and bras. We had come in the entrance that led directly to ladies' underwear.

Poor Phra Suthee seemed to be paralysed, his eyes glued to the floor as though his life, his honour and his purity depended on it. "Oh.... oh... oh...", he kept saying. A lady customer nearby picked up a black, frilly thing from a counter and held it against herself. "Oh.. oh.. oh..." Unfortunately I burst out laughing at his obvious embarrassment, as did several young lady customers and finally I actually had to take hold of his arm and lead him through the department, since, by then, his eyes were tightly closed. He didn't open them again until we were safely out of moral danger in the stationery department.

As it turned out, Fairyland was a very ordinary, average-sized department store, but I realised that for my mostly poor students it was very aptly named. The store was full of Western or Western-style consumer goods: TVs, home computers, videos, beautiful clothes, furniture and all the rest; the things most of my students could only dream about, but few would ever attain to.

I don't think Phra Suthee ever quite forgave me for taking him to the store but, in a roundabout way, he did get his own back.

The visit became a standing joke between us and we would often make schoolboy-level references to his reactions in the underwear department. One evening soon after our visit, I was sitting on the balcony of my kuti when a little novice arrived with several cartons of milk, a gift from Phra Suthee, he said. My friend and I would often share the small gifts of 'special' food that laypeople offered. I told the novice to thank Phra Suthee and to tell him I looked forward to seeing him in ladies' underwear again soon. The novice looked at me as though as I was very weird (which is the usual way the novices look at me) and off he went.

Next morning I met Phra Suthee on our way to the Bote for morning chanting. "Thanks for the milk", I said. "What milk?", he asked, quite mystified. "The milk the novice delivered last night. He said it was from you, from Phra Suthee". "Oh", replied my friend, as realisation dawned. "He meant from Phra Suthee Thammasopon, the abbot". The abbot. The Abbot! I had sent a message to the abbot to say I wanted to see him in ladies' underwear? Aaarrgh.!!!

Chapter 26

For anybody who plans or needs to stay in Thailand longer than most visitors, it is essential to learn how Thai people reckon time. In my own experience most Thais really don't have much sense of time at all and are nearly always late for appointments, (sometimes by several days) and rarely understand why many Westerners find this irritating. In Bangkok, of course, the traffic can usually be blamed, and is, and frequently with good reason.

I decided I had to learn how to tell the time Thai-style following an experience which cost me greatly. I received a letter in Nakhon Sawan informing me that I had to be at a certain temple in Bangkok on a particular date, in fact it was that very day, for the letter had been delayed in the postal system for nearly a week.

At that time, I had a looksit who could speak fairly good English but he had the habit of thinking in Thai and then translating word for word into English, with the consequence that his manner of speaking was sometimes either extremely odd, extremely funny or occasionally very misleading and sometimes all three at the same time (which is exactly how I speak Thai).

On receipt of the letter early in the morning, I threw it and a few changes of under-robes into a bag and my looksit and I dashed off to the bus station, forgetting that it was a special holiday and that all the buses were therefore fully booked. We jumped into a taxi and went to a private coach company, but they were also fully booked. Another taxi took us the several miles to Nakhon Sawan railway station and we arrived there at about 10.45 am.

I was sure trains to Bangkok were fairly frequent so I sent my looksit off to the booking office to buy tickets for the next available train. When he came back with the tickets, I asked him what time the train would arrive in Nakhon Sawan. He thought for a moment and replied, "5 o'clock". "What!" I exclaimed in disbelief. "That's more than six hours! I haven't got time to wait that long" and without giving him the chance to say anything else, I swept out of the station, impatiently demanding he find me an aeroplane, or at the very least a taxi.

Nakhon Sawan doesn't have an airport but the taxi we had arrived in was still parked outside the station and I negotiated a price for the 240 kilometre ride to Bangkok. This was about 20 times the rail fare, plus a bit extra of course because I was a foreigner. I was desperate to get to Bangkok and had no alternative but to agree to the price.

When we were finally on our way, I managed to get both my irritation and my hunger under control. I hadn't eaten breakfast and by then had missed lunch as well. Seeing that it was reasonably safe to speak, my looksit asked politely, "Why was Luang Por 'jai rorn', hot heart (impatient) to wait for the train?" Thinking he was an idiot, I slowly and calmly explained that we arrived at the station just before 11 am and the train was due at 5 pm and therefore we would have to wait six hours. Thai trains, even those mysteriously called 'Express' are sometimes incredibly slow and the journey from Nakhon Sawan to Bangkok can take six hours, nearly twice as long as the bus so, I explained, we would not actually arrive at the temple I needed to go to until the following day.

He was quiet for a moment while he absorbed this logic and then said: "But we only needed to wait ten minutes". I looked at him in astonishment. "Ten minutes? But you told me the train was at 5 o' clock!" "Yes, that's right", he said " Har mong—five o'clock". I understood. 'Har mong' in Thai does indeed translate literally as 5 o' clock, but 5 o'clock to the Thai is 11 am by Western reckoning!

The Thais split the clock into four periods and start counting from six. 6 am Western time is also 6 Thai time, but 7 am becomes 1, 8 am becomes 2, 9 am becomes 3, 10 am becomes 4, 11 am becomes 5 and 12 is noon (but it can also be 12). Similarly in the evening quarter, 6 pm is 6 but 7 pm becomes 1, 8 pm becomes 2, and so on. There is an additional word to make it clear which part of the day is meant but the word is often omitted in speech, if it seems obvious. In fact, the Thai system of telling the time does have its own sort of logic but it takes a while to get used to. It always seems especially odd to me that most Thai clocks have Roman numerals but a Thai asked the time will still look at the clock, on which the hour hand is quite clearly pointing at 9, and say "three".

My lack of understanding of all this cost me about 4,000 baht for taxis and I decided then that it was time to learn to tell the time Thai-style. It actually cost me more than 4,000 baht for in my impatience to get out of the station and into a taxi, I left my bag behind on the plat-form, together with the letter which told me the address of the temple in Bangkok, so we never actually got there anyway. As soon as we reached Bangkok, we simply turned round and came back again, ar-riving at about 7.30 pm—or was it half past one?

Time in most monasteries in still regulated to a certain extent by the ringing of bells or the beating of drums, signals which ad-vise, warn or command. At Wat Nahoob, I had the job of ringing the bell at the top of the bell tower for morning and evening chant-ing. Another bell was used to remind us it was lunch time. Another very small hand-bell was rung to call us to special services in the Bote, such as ordinations.

It is a tradition in Thai monasteries that during the Pansa an addi-tional call is made at dusk to warn any monks outside the monastery that they must return immediately, since a monk must be within the monastery boundaries every night of the Rains Retreat.

At Wat Nahoob, the new monks had the job of sounding this warning but it was done on huge old drums, kept in the sala, not from the bell tower. The idea at Nahoob seemed to be to make as much noise as possible, and the aesthetic value of the performance was of secondary importance. The few monks who were staying at the monastery for the Pansa would gather round the huge ancient drums to listen. This made the exercise somewhat pointless since we were all very obviously present. Nevertheless, the young monks would enthusiastically beat not only the drums but would also bang large saucepans together, and sometimes bits of wood, which culminated in the most terrible racket.

At most monasteries I believe the evening call is of one of two kinds, either similar to Wat Nahoob's or the straight-forward, sonorous beat of a drum or the ringing of a bell. At Wat Kob we are considerably more sophisticated and the novices who have the duty have turned the evening call into a musical art form, albeit one that can only be described as 'free expression'.

Our two enormous and ancient drums are kept at the top of the bell tower, which also houses four bells of different sizes, all of them big. The bell tower is at least twice the height of Wat Nahoob's, ensuring that whatever sounds emanate therefrom are sure to be heard over the whole of the city.

The Abbot of Wat Kob is usually a stickler for doing things by the book, but he seems quite happy to turn a blind eye, or at least a deaf ear, to the novices' nightly performance. And it is a performance well worth hearing and one which I always look forward to.

It usually starts off without any build-up or warning with a great drum roll which lasts a couple of minutes but which then quite suddenly and surprisingly stops. This is followed by a long silence which builds up the suspense as to what might happen next. (In fact, one of the novices told me that they use this couple of minutes to decide what they will do next, since each evening's performance is always a bit different). A single 'ding' on one of the smaller bells often heralds the next phase. A drum beat, slow as a heart beat, booms out and after a few beats is joined by a bell, rung once between every half dozen or so drum beats. Very gradually, the drum beat becomes faster and then is joined by another drum with a different tone. A second bell joins in and then quite suddenly all hell breaks lose at the top of the tower as the drum beats rain down at an incredible speed. A sudden stop and a long silence and then, again, the single 'ding' which heralds a second phase. This continues for about 20 minutes, each sequence becoming faster and faster, until finally all the bells and drums are in use at the same time making a noise which, although perhaps not best described as 'music', is certainly impressive.

Although the novices involved have a fantastic sense of timing and rhythm, their sense of tone is somewhat lacking, or maybe it's just a warped sense of humour. One of the great bells obviously has a crack or fault in it. Just as the performance seems to have come to an end, there is often a single note struck on the faulty bell, a quite hideous note unknown on any musical scale. It's as awful as finger-nails on a blackboard. It makes me both wince and burst out laughing every time! But any monk outside of the monastery boundary definitely gets the message to come home.

Bells are also used at Wat Kob during the Rains Retreat to waken the monks at 4 am. I often do get up at that time to take a quiet early morning walk around the monastery grounds, though I have yet to see any other monk up and about.

I don't think anybody who knows the Thais, and even the Thai people themselves, would dispute the fact that they have the most amazing ability to sleep. Any time, anywhere and in any position. I once asked a lady, on her first visit to Thailand, what her initial impression of the country was: "Everybody's asleep", she said. And when I ask students what their favourite pastimes are, 'sleeping' is invariably top of the list.

The most graphic example I've ever seen of this ability to sleep was a young monk paying his respects to an Abbot. Junior monks frequently bow three times to their seniors with what is known as a 'five-point prostration'. The bow, or graab, starts from the kneeling position, sitting on the heels, and the upper body is lowered until the elbows, palms and forehead are touching the floor. The senior monk was sitting on his mat and the young monk approached on his knees, sat back on his heels and gracefully and mindfully made his first bow. He raised himself back to his kneeling position and then made the second bow, equally as gracefully. And then the third, but after the third bow he didn't raise himself up. He stayed where he was, his forehead resting on the floor, fast asleep. I was amazed at this, but the Abbot didn't react at all. He sat for a few moments and then quietly got up and walked away, leaving the young monk to continue his sleep.

At Wat Kob we had a very nice young monk who was much like Giant at Wat Nahoob, not quite fat, but big and soft-looking and with a lovely smile. He had the legendary reputation of being a very serious sleeper even by Thai standards and the other monks claimed he spent far more time asleep than awake. I didn't really believe this until I started to get to know him a little and observed him. It was quite true. He slept through morning chanting, he slept through evening chanting, he slept through ordination ceremonies and through funeral services and I had even seen him sleep through lunch at a layperson's house. During services he would sit perfectly upright, hands raised to chest level with his palms together, and only his closed eyes and occasionally nodding head would indicate that he wasn't entirely with us.

Although it happened before I went to live at Wat Kob, the other monks still laughed about an incident concerning the sleepy monk. Apparently there was a very long service in the Bote when all 40 or so monks and novices were sitting in a long line on a specially-built platform which raised them about three feet above the assembled laypeople. The platform was about a yard wide but unfortunately the back of it was not against a wall. During the chanting, the sleepy monk, sitting with his legs folded to one side, hands in the prayer-like attitude, began to nod off. Gradually his body started to lean backwards, further and further, until quite suddenly and with a great crash he fell off the back of the platform and disappeared, much to the consternation of the laypeople, the horror of the Abbot and the absolute delight of the novices who collapsed in laughing heaps at this unexpected and welcome interruption to an otherwise long and boring service. I wish I could have been there!

Chapter 27

When a man ordains, there is absolutely no commitment made to remain as a monk for a specified period and he is free to leave the Sangha, to disrobe, at any time. Many men do have a fixed period in mind when they ordain, especially if they are ordaining to 'make merit' for their family, or a departed loved one. This may vary from only a week or so, to several months.

The disrobing ceremony is short, but the first time I witnessed it I found it extremely poignant, though that was probably due to the particular circumstances involved. A young man of about 25 ordained at Wat Kob when his father died. The young monk could speak some English and I had several conversations with him. Unusually for a Thai, he was a very withdrawn and intense individual, but extremely likeable. It was clear he took his ordination seriously, even though he knew it was temporary. He totally believed in the idea of transferring merit to the deceased in the hope that he would have a better re-birth. He was determined to do the best he could for his father. The company for which he worked allowed male staff three months ordination leave, so he decided to ordain for that period.

He walked on binderbaht with the abbot and me each morning and I also observed him frequently during the various ceremonies we attended together. Of all the 'temporary' monks I have ever seen, and I have seen many hundreds, he was undoubtedly the most perfectly behaved and I believe his behaviour was not just 'show' or outward form. The Vinaya training rules about deportment and every other aspect of behaviour seemed to come perfectly naturally to him. His whole attitude towards his new status as a monk seemed to me to be one of total sincerity.

Many young Thai men who ordain seem to do so with the attitude that it is something that has to be endured, almost like national service. Since they were little boys, they have known that when they reached the age of twenty or so, their parents expected them to ordain and they have come to accept it as part of their gradual passing from youth to adulthood. I don't think that's necessarily a bad thing, particularly if they ordain with a positive attitude, but sadly many do not. In common with laypeople of all religions, many people in Thailand claim to be Buddhist without really giving much thought to what that means and often without having any great interest or involvement in the religion beyond a few simple cycle-of-life ceremonies. But I don't think there can be as much social pressure on young men of any other religion to become so directly involved, whether they like it or not. Frequently in Thailand when young men ordain they shave their heads and put on the robe but those often seem to be the only changes. Providing they can fill in the form, have no obvious physical or mental defects and have a guarantor, there is nothing to stop them from becoming monks and fulfilling their social or family obligations. Consequently we have all types of young men ordaining and they often bring into the Sangha all sorts of bad habits and vices. Judging by their behaviour, some, I am sure, would benefit more from a period in prison than in a monastery.

This particular young monk spent his three months studying Dhamma, the Vinaya and meditation and I was able to witness the changes in him even over a short period. He frequently sought out the most senior monks at Wat Kob to talk about the Buddha's teaching and slowly his whole demeanour became one of confident calmness. Sometimes after a meditation period, his face seemed almost to glow. There was something about him that was definitely different from any other monk I have met. Others noticed it too and I had the feeling that he was exactly the sort of person who could not only benefit himself by living within the Sangha but could benefit the Sangha also.

On the day of his disrobement 22 monks, including the abbot, assembled in the Bote. It is actually up to the monk disrobing how many monks are present to witness the ceremony. In fact, none apart from the abbot are strictly necessary, but the young monk had made so many friends and impressed so many of the other monks that we all wanted to be there to wish him luck by chanting a traditional Pali blessing for him.

The monks sat in two lines, on the left and right-hand sides of the abbot, forming a corridor through which the young monk approached the abbot on his knees, his Sangghati or extra robe folded over his left shoulder. He bowed before the abbot and quietly chanted the Namo three times. He was then supposed to make a simple statement in Pali which translates as "I give up the training. May you henceforth regard me as a layman". His voice faltered part way through. He stopped and looked at the abbot. The abbot looked kindly at him but did not intervene in whatever thoughts were going through the young monk's mind. The thoughts in my mind were "Don't say it, don't do it!" but nobody may interfere or try to influence another's decision in this matter. He sat quite still for a few moments and the silence and tension in the Bote were almost tangible. I could imagine his mind torn between the life of a monk, which he quite certainly found deeply satisfying, and that of a layman... his family and friends, his career, perhaps a young lady waiting somewhere.

Finally he continued the Pali stanza, sadly removed his Sangghati and passed it to the abbot who directed him to leave the assembly to change from his robes into 'normal' clothes. When he returned, he took the Five Precepts of a layperson and the abbot splashed consecrated water over his head and shoulders, while the rest of us chanted a blessing wishing him good fortune in his new life. I, for one, meant every word, though I found the chanting difficult because of the lump in my throat.

I have heard several stories about longer-term monks who for various reasons have decided to disrobe, but when it actually came to the moment they were entirely unable to make the statement that declared their intention to return to lay life. They have stayed as monks.

I have also personally known of long-term monks who have disrobed and then almost immediately wished they hadn't. In some cases they have soon re-ordained, even though disrobing nullifies all the years they had already spent in the robes. A monk's 'age', or seniority, is measured by the number of Pansas he has lived as a monk in a continuous period. If a monk with, for example, 20 Pansas disrobed and then re-ordained, his previous 20 years do not count. He would be a junior monk again and even a monk with only one Pansa would theoretically be his senior.

Once when I was visiting Wat Mahadhatu, a man came into Section 5 and smiled in recognition when he saw me. He was wearing jeans, a tee-shirt and a leather jacket and it wasn't until he spoke to me that I realised he was one of my old teacher-monks from London. I had never seen him with hair or street clothes before and totally failed to recognise him, though I knew him well. He had returned to Thailand and disrobed but he was finding lay life quite difficult. He had originally become a novice when he was about eight years old, ordained as a monk at 20 and remained so for about 17 years. He actually therefore knew little or nothing about the 'real' world or how to cope with it. Although he was a Maha and very skilled at chanting, that isn't a lot of help when looking for a job and he was finding it difficult to get anything other than fairly menial work.

Besides the practical difficulty of being untrained and unprepared for living and working in the lay world there is often another great difficulty for the long-term monk who disrobes. For many years, he has been in the highest social position in Thailand and may have become quite used to receiving great respect from everybody he comes into contact with — people prostrating before him, crawling around on their hands and knees and generally being at his beck and call. The monk, theoretically at least, is in a higher social position than HM the King. A monk does not bow to the King: the King bows to the monk. For the long-term monk who has become accustomed to his high social standing, it must sometimes be extremely difficult to adjust to a new role, that of just another layman. In Thailand people are frequently categorised socially and respected by others depending on their wealth, standard of education and the outward forms of success. The long-term monk who disrobes may have none of these and finds himself suddenly at the bottom of the social heap instead of the top.

Many young Thai men ordain for two or three years and it is often they who really benefit from the Buddha's teaching. They have lived as monks long enough to understand something of the Dhamma and then want to live a less reclusive live in the outside world, applying that understanding to their lives as laymen. But it doesn't always work out that way. At Wat Kob we had a young monk who was extremely handsome, though slightly less than bright. He had been a monk for two or three Pansas when he met a beautiful girl who told him she was in love with him. He disrobed with the intention of marrying her but as soon as she saw him in ordinary clothes, her passion dissipated and she rejected him! She only loved him as a monk. He reordained soon after, and seemed to have lost all interest in women.

The second disrobing ceremony I was invited to attend affected me as much as the first, though in a different way and for a different reason. A week before the start of my fourth Pansa, my good friend Phra Suthee decided he'd had enough and announced his decision to disrobe. He had been a monk for nearly six years, but had never really wanted to be. Before ordaining, he had a good career with the Ports Authority of Thailand. He was halfway through an open university course, working towards a BA in Public Administration, and according to him, he had a very active and full social life. He told me that he was enjoying himself immensely but his parents were having some difficulty with their lives and felt they needed someone to 'make merit' for them. They asked him to become a monk and he reluctantly agreed, but without telling them of his reluctance. That may sound very odd to a Westerner, but young Thai people usually have a very high level of respect for their parents and older people generally and will follow their parents' instructions even when, as in this case, it goes against their own wishes.

Phra Suthee informed the abbot that he wanted to disrobe and the abbot set a date a few days later in that week. Nobody ever seems either surprised or disappointed when a monk announces his intention to leave the Sangha and Phra Suthee told me that the abbot didn't even ask why he wanted to disrobe. My friend invited me and four other monks to be present at the short ceremony in the abbot's kuti.

The day before the ceremony, Phra Suthee and I went into town to buy clothes, since his old clothes had long since been given or thrown away. He needed trousers, shirts, underclothes, shoes, everything, in fact.

Before ordaining, I really used to enjoy shopping for clothes and would usually buy something new to wear almost every week. I didn't buy extremely expensive clothes, but they were always well-designed, well-cut and reasonably stylish. I liked clothes. I liked buying them and I liked wearing them. They were, I suppose, just 'ego props', a way of announcing to the rest of the world what sort of person I was, or at least considered myself to be.

The store that we chose to shop at had some very nice clothes indeed and as I helped Phra Suthee go through the racks of shirts and trousers, I totally forgot that I was supposed to be helping him chose and instead started to evaluate the various colours and styles for myself to wear. I usually don't have any money, so even buying a pair of socks would be out of the question, but I could picture myself in that jacket, or this shirt. I rarely give a thought to my life before I ordained but just seeing those lovely clothes led me on to thinking about the sort of occasions that I might wear such clothes, which in turn led me on to remembering the enjoyment I used to have in my old life: a lot of it was superficial, but it was enjoyable nevertheless.

I started to become quite melancholy and for a moment, I actually found myself thinking about my own possible disrobement. When I ordained, I was fairly sure that I would remain a monk for the rest of my life, but I've learned enough to know that people change constantly, that we never know what the future might hold and that there should never be any regrets about the past or fixed plans for the future. Disrobing has never been on my agenda, but the mind can constantly surprise with its fickleness, despite any attempts to train it.

My melancholy wasn't helped by suddenly catching sight of myself in a full-length mirror. It may sound strange, but I hadn't looked at myself in a mirror since the day I ordained. I use a very small mirror everyday to shave, but then I am concentrating on the task in hand and do not see my face as a whole and certainly not my whole body. What I saw in the mirror was a shock. A very tall, very thin, pale, bald and ageing man, wearing a hideously-bright orange robe which came only to his knees, with skinny arms and legs sticking out. I'm quite surprised the mirror didn't shatter, for it was not a pretty sight, but I quickly reminded myself that such a judgement based on my physical appearance was purely ego, vanity, and really of no great importance. My life was no longer concerned, or should not be concerned, with such trivial matters.

Trivial matters ... Phra Suthee was asking me whether I preferred the pale green shirt or the dark blue one, and was this tie suitable for that style of collar? A couple of laywomen, Phra Suthee's supporters, joined us at the store. We spent a couple of hours trying to decide whether slip-on or lace-up shoes were best, and then the style, and then the colour, and then the price. We went backwards and forwards between racks of shoes and sandals. Just watching and listening to the three of them discussing, so seriously, how best to cover Phra Suthee's body with cloth and leather was a good reminder about how shallow so much of lay life is. Thoughts of disrobing slipped away.

Mr Suthee came to visit me a couple of times after he disrobed. He was working as a cashier in a petrol station and he seemed quite happy, though I couldn't really see how he could be. He earned little money and had little time off and what he had was spent sleeping. It seemed to me that somehow his life didn't seem to have any point or direction. But he looked very smart.

Chapter 28

It is a fact that a lot of Thai people don't seem to take me very seriously as a monk and I have heard other Phra Farang say they have met with similar 'resistance'. Despite wearing the same robes, shaving my head and following the same rules as my Thai colleagues, I am still not a 'real' monk. This isn't a problem for me, if anything it is amusing, though mysterious.

When I have occasionally asked why I am not taken seriously, I am always told: "You are not Thai and you do not chant". I point out gently that the Buddha wasn't Thai either and as far as I know, he didn't have a lot to say about the necessity or efficacy of chanting. It doesn't make any difference. I have got used to the fact that I am an oddity. Thai people like to come and have a look at me and although they usually show the outward forms of respect, it is obvious they don't really know what to make of me. But I do get on well with most Thai people I meet.

When I first went to live at Wat Kob, I felt at least some of the monks had the same attitude. They were interested in this strange new species that had arrived in their midst and although they had heard that such beings existed, I don't think any of them ever expected to meet one. At one time, there was a rumour circulating in the monastery that I was a spy for the Supreme Patriarch; another version labelled me as a spy for the Pope! Sometimes if I came upon a group of monks in deep discussion, they would fall silent until I had passed by. Perhaps they suspected that I had a microphone hidden under my robe. Happily we seemed to pass that stage after a few months and I think generally they do accept me now, or at least tolerate me.

Although to many Thais I will never be a real monk in their terms, there are some people who do take me very seriously and who make great effort to ensure I am happy and comfortable at Wat Kob so that I can practise in my own peculiar Western way. Chief amongst these, luckily for me, is the abbot. If he didn't think I was 'serious' in my practice, I don't think I would be welcome to stay, since I am much more of a liability to the monastery than an asset. Although I never complain about anything, since I really have nothing to complain about, the abbot goes out of his way to ensure that I am sabbai at his monastery.

The temple boys who live below my kuti think I am a little weird, but we generally get along fine. However, they are noisy and I occasionally have to rebuke them about it. One evening, I was sitting on my balcony, talking with a schoolteacher and her husband. At the time, I was helping the teacher with an English sociology course that she was preparing for her students at the teacher training college in the city. The temple boys' radios were going full blast, doors were slamming and they were laughing, shouting, singing and generally behaving in a perfectly normal manner for teenage boys.

The teacher asked me if I didn't find the kuti very noisy. I said it was usually OK but the boys were sometimes a disturbance late in the evening when I usually did a couple of hours of meditation. Nothing more was said.

At the time, the old Bote was being renovated. It was to have a new tiled roof, a new marble floor, cooling fans, mosquito screens and a number of other necessary repairs. It could no longer be used for religious services because any monastery can have only one Bote and the old one had been 'decommissioned' when the new Bote had been completed some years before. It was a beautiful, cool and very peaceful building; its 18-inch- thick, ancient walls admitted hardly any sound. But the monastery really had no specific use for it.

Soon after the renovation was completed, the abbot came to see me and to my great surprise, presented me with the key to the building. He said he had heard that my kuti was sometimes too noisy for meditation and he was 'giving' me the old Bote as my personal meditation chamber. He added that if I wanted, I could live there and treat it as my kuti and he was having a shower and 'Western-style' toilet built at one side of it for my use. I was overwhelmed by his kindness and I have made use of the old Bote for meditation many times, and frequently sleep in it.

On another occasion, I decided to try to do something about the state of my toilet and shower, which were in a sort of concrete shed behind my kuti. Each of the three old kutis had a similar arrangement; a shed containing two showers and two toilets, one for the monk and the other for the dek wats who lived below his kuti. The tin roofs leaked, the doors were hanging off and they were very unpleasant, despite our efforts to keep them clean.

A friend had sent me a little money from England and I decided to use it to buy paint and some new corrugated tin for the roof. The abbot will not allow any atlerations to any part of the monastry without his permission, so one evening as we were leaving the Bote after chanting I asked him if it would be OK for me to carry out this mini-renovation. "No", he said, and he walked away.

I was quite taken back by this and assumed that, as usual, the abbot hadn't understood me, but I was even more surprised when, a few days later, builders arrived and completely gutted all three shower blocks and then entirely refurbished them, as new.

I didn't know at the time, that both the renovation of the old Bote and the rebuilding of the showers were paid for almost entirely by a businessman named Khun Opas and his family. He was the husband of the teacher whom I had helped produce the English sociology course. The abbot is much admired in Nakhon Sawan for what he has achieved at Wat Kob and I think his greatest admirer must be Khun Opas. For me, he epitomised Thai 'jai dee', good heart.

As I hadn't needed to use my friend's gift of money to renovate my toilet and shower, I decided to find out how much it would cost to have mosquito screens fitted to the doors and windows of my kuti.

Mosquitos have never been a bother to me but whenever it rained, my kuti would be invaded by literally thousands of flying ants and they were a nuisance. I hadn't a clue what mosquito screens cost or whether I had sufficient money and I asked Khun Opas to arrange an estimate. The next day, a man came to measure up and the following day the screens were fitted, not only to my kuti but also to my looksit's room downstairs. I was horribly embarrassed about this because I thought there had been a misunderstanding and I would now have to afford it, regardless of the cost. But no, Khun Opas had already paid the bill and I never did find out what that was. I told him I wasn't very happy about this but he explained that he hadn't given the screens to me personally; they were for the kuti and for anybody who might live there. He was in effect donating them to the monastery, in which case I was delighted to accept them and thanked him on behalf of all the monks who might live in my kuti in the future.

Every monastery in Thailand needs material support and every monastery has its supporters: people who either give of their own money or who are active in raising money from others. Khun Opas does both, but in a quiet way and, I believe, without thought of 'making merit'. He does it simply because he has 'jai dee' and a genuine and deep respect for Luang Por Suthee. And his 'jai dee' does not extend only to lavish building programmes, for every Thursday without fail, he will be waiting bare-footed outside the monastery gates early in the morning, and he will offer food to each monk as he passes on his binderbaht round.

I have been lucky to meet several people like Khun Opas while living at Wat Kob. I don't 'cultivate' such people, of course, but they are always welcome to visit me at my kuti if they want to practise their English conversation a little. All my visitors are associates or friends of teachers that I have worked with and I think most of them are university graduates. Most are able to speak good or very good English. Some seem to have quite a different attitude to Buddhism to many other Thai people I have met.

A teacher and her husband invited me to lunch at their house on Christmas Day. Unusually the invitation was for me alone, rather than for a chapter of nine monks. I was delighted to accept, though I nervously dreaded that I would have to chant a solo Pali blessing after the meal.

My Christmas dinner was pizza, French fries, Christmas cake and apples, eaten alone while the rest of the family sat around the TV watching a video of 'Jurassic Park'. I had worked on the fringes of the film industry for a while and am a great admirer of Steven Spielberg, so I didn't know whether to mindfully eat my pizza or mindfully watch the dinosaurs. The pizza won, since I rarely have the opportunity to eat 'farang food'. When I had finished eating, I placed my hands together to give a blessing. "Oh, don't worry about that", said the teacher, "we follow Buddhism as a philosophy, not as a religion". I lowered my hands in amazement and instead of a Pali blessing, simply offered my very sincere thanks for their kindness.

Back at the monastery, I told another monk about this and he was highly critical of me for not giving the usual blessing. He could well have been right, I really don't know.

I actually get on well with the other monks as far as I know, but in a neutral sort of way. Few of us can communicate but the monks I especially admire, generally the most senior ones, tend not to be especially communicative anyway. I learn a lot just by being with them and observing and some are much like my old teachers at Wat Buddhapadipa.

One senior monk came out with a small pearl of wisdom that I have never forgotten. Nine of us were sitting in the back of a pick-up waiting to be taken somewhere or other when a chatty new monk, seeking to be friendly, said something to me in Thai which I didn't understand at all. He turned to the other monks and said: "Mai ruu reuang", "He doesn't know what's going on". The senior monk then turned to him and said: "Mai ruu reuang: sabbai", a Thai idiom meaning "When you don't know what's going on you are content". For me that has really proven to be the case.

Monks are just people; many are seriously trying to rise above what makes 'ordinary' mortals 'tick', but I think only a very few succeed to any great extent. I suppose any group of people, monks or laymen, adults or children, can become 'cliquey', especially when they live together in fairly confined quarters. Individuals may squabble amongst themselves; one bunch doesn't like the other bunch; they gossip about how bad that one is, or how well that one practises etc. I expect this goes on at Wat Kob as much as anywhere else but I don't know a thing about it and therefore cannot be involved. Nobody asks me for my opinion; I cannot take sides in squabbles or personality conflicts, I am not part of any clique. I am almost entirely isolated and that suits me fine.

An English monk once told me of his experience living in a Thai monastery. He said: "You can be 'one of', but you cannot be 'one off'. My own experience is quite different. I am 'one off' because not only am I the only Phra Farang at Wat Kob but I am also the only one in the entire province. And I am not 'one of' because I don't chant and the other monks understand that I do not want to speak or socialise very much, not because I don't like my colleagues but simply because I don't feel any need to. Hence, for a time, I had the nickname 'one-man show', which I don't think was an insult by any means but was merely a reflection of my self-imposed, solitary status.

I understand enough Thai now to ask any questions I need to ask, there's always the chance I might be understood and to comply with any instructions I am given. And that's all I need to know. I enjoy the occasional chat in English with my visitors but they also know that I really do not want to socialise at any great length and they visit for short times and infrequently.

I get on with my own practice in my own way with, I think, my abbot's blessing, and that's all I do. I frequently haven't the faintest idea of what's going on. And I am sabbai.

Chapter 29

Many years ago, Acharn Amara Thera told me that after I ordained, I should wander around Thailand, "looking in every cave and at the foot of every tree", until I found my spiritual guide.

Although Acharn Amara Thera had taught me, I think he knew from his long experience that he was not necessarily *the* teacher for me; he was not the teacher who would eventually lead me to the 'goal' of my meditation practice. His great wisdom and experience had been the starting point but if any student really wants to progress towards the highest reaches of meditation, he may often need a guide to whom he can relate at a very deep and special level; an intuitive rather than an intellectual level.

The guide needs to be able to understand the limits of his student and to be able to push him gently, and sometimes perhaps not so gently, in certain directions, with subtle advice that does not lead the student into expectation but allows him genuinely to experience and know for himself. Sometimes these things can neither be put into words nor taught, but must be intuitively self-realised.

I haven't wandered around Thailand looking for my teacher-guide and as a consequence, I am sure I have made many mistakes in my meditation practice. Perhaps I am still making them. I know at times I have been side-tracked but I believe I have usually managed to get myself back on the right course, or what I think of as the right course for me.

When I first moved to Wat Kob, I wasn't entirely sure if I was practising my meditation in the most productive way. I was still usually practising two or three hours of walking and sitting meditation everyday but I was never forcing myself to sit at pre-set times. This was generally satisfactory, but despite that, I felt the meditation itself was becoming almost routine. It is at such times that every practitioner really needs a teacher-guide, but apart from some scholarly books about meditation, I didn't have a guide and had to rely on my own feelings about the direction I should take. I decided to break the routine and add new elements to my meditation; to experiment a little.

I first started to undertake continuous twelve-hour sittings and then later, on just three occasions, continuous 24-hour sittings. I totally emptied one of the rooms in my kuti and had my looksit, Banjob, lock the door from the outside. Since I couldn't get out of the room, I could neither eat nor drink, urinate, defecate or anything else. I did not sleep. I just sat in meditation. I wanted to observe the body and its physical needs over a long period and see what degree of control could be exercised over those needs. The latter wasn't particularly important, though it was interesting. At the end of the pre-arranged period Banjob would open the door to let me out. These sessions were quite useful and although mentally I didn't find them too much of a strain, unfortunately physically they didn't do me any good at all. During the last of the 24-hour sittings, my knee cartilage was damaged again and although that gave me the unwelcome opportunity to meditate on acute physical discomfort, it marked the end of the 'marathons'.

I also took to meditating in the oven of the monastery's crematorium. For those who are as yet unfamiliar with such ovens, Wat Kob's is basically a brick chamber about seven feet long and two feet six inches wide. There are two such ovens in the crematorium, side by side. In each, the walls curve upwards and towards each other to make an arch shape which is about four feet six inches high in the middle. Not high enough to stand up in, but I don't suppose many people need to.

Many cremations are held at Wat Kob, hence the need for two ovens, and rarely a week goes by without at least a couple of funerals being held. Sometimes both ovens are in use at the same time and therefore don't have much opportunity to cool down.

The first time I decided to meditate in the oven, I nearly gave up after a few minutes. Although neither oven had been used that day, the heat inside was almost unbearable. The bricks had retained heat from the cremation the day before and were actually hot to touch. Because of the narrow width, I was unable to sit facing the door and had to sit sideways, with my back against one wall and my knees pressed against the opposite wall. My back and knees were roasting within minutes and sweat was literally pouring from me.

The oven seemed to be almost airless, though some air entered through the ash chamber beneath. The air was foul and stank of death. That may sound fanciful, but I have been close enough to week-old corpses to recognise the smell; an oily and musty stench that catches in the throat and which not only seemed to cling to my skin but also permeated my robes, even after a short time.

The first night I used the oven as a meditation chamber, I told Banjob to stand 'sentry' on the crematorium steps while I was inside. He absolutely hated the idea because like many Thai people he is terrified of ghosts, but I needed him there to allay my own fears. I wasn't frightened of ghosts; I was worried that someone may have come and turned the big wheels that lock the thick, steel door, or even do a 'test firing' of the oven, though why anybody should I can't imagine.

I also needed Banjob to shut the heavy door after I climbed into the chamber and to open it at the end of the pre-set period of one hour: not surprisingly, there is no handle on the inside and it was extremely difficult to push open in the cramped quarters.

On the first occasion I climbed in and Banjob pushed the door shut and scarpered. He ran back to his room, fully intending to return at the end of an hour but, in the nature of Thai people, fell asleep instead. I had no clock with me in the oven (and anyway it was totally black in there) and had no idea of the time, but I eventually realised that considerably more than an hour had passed. With great difficulty I squirmed about in the oven until I could get into a position to push the door open.

It was an uncanny piece of timing, for at that very moment, an old Thai gentleman was walking past the crematorium and nearly died of fright when the oven door slowly opened and a pale, sooty, zombie crawled out!

At first, I didn't tell any of the other monks that I was using the oven as a meditation chamber because they might conceivably have thought I was, well, mad I suppose. But of course, word eventually got around and much to my surprise, several other monks wanted to join me for these 'bake-ins', as they became known.

There was what seemed a genuine purpose to this apparently bizarre behaviour. One theme of meditation is to contemplate corpses in various succeeding stages of decomposition and to understand, to genuinely know, that there is no escape for any of us from such a condition. Everybody accepts intellectually that the physical body will die and will be buried or burned, but that's not entirely the point. To reflect upon the impermanence of the physical body can change the way we view not only our own and other bodies but also our reactions to other people and everything around us. It can prompt a new way of evaluating ourselves and others and our 'role' in life now, whilst we are still able to do something about it. That won't stop the physical body from dying of course, but it can greatly improve the quality of this life and lessen much of the suffering that we inflict upon ourselves.

The Buddha recommended that his monks undertake such meditation on the impermanent nature of the body, on death and therefore on 'life' in charnel grounds. He specified corpses in nine succeeding stages of decomposition as suitable objects for meditation. I suppose in India in those days there were many places where corpses could be seen, but not in modern Thailand. Although I frequently see corpses during my normal duty at funerals, it is not possible to spend much time with them, usually only a few moments and certainly not the several days needed to watch the changes that take place in the body.

I thought at the time the nearest I could get to a charnel ground as an environment for this sort of meditation was the crematorium oven.

It was after one of these sittings that I realised a couple of things. The monk in the other oven, Phra Acharn Perm, had been a monk for about eight years. He was a Dhamma teacher at the monastery school and was also a very serious and experienced meditator, who worked hard to extend his understanding. At the end of two hours, our little alarm clock rang to indicate the end of the sitting, though sometimes we would ignore it and each of us would continue until our meditation had reached a natural conclusion. On that occasion, we slowly and quietly changed our positions, moving as mindfully as possible. I climbed out of my oven and adjusted my wet robe. We did not look at each other. We did not need to speak. There was no "how was it for you?" type of chatter. We didn't need to analyse or compare notes. We walked slowly away from the crematorium to our kutis.

As I wearily climbed my kuti steps, I knew, without any doubt, that at some time in the last few months, I had passed an important stage in my meditation practice. I believed there had come some point when I had built up a sufficiently solid foundation of understanding to carry me forward, each cautious, new step seeming logical and natural. I had, in a sense, developed my own momentum, albeit a slow and sometimes faltering one.

This was nothing to do with meditating in the oven, for I soon realised that the crematorium was just a place, a very hot and smelly place. Although my meditation there had been satisfying and helpful, without a corpse, it was a poor substitute for a charnel ground.

Soon after one of the 'bake-ins', I was in the meditation sala of Wat Kob's mango garden. Around the walls were posters of famous Thai meditation masters and also photographs of dead bodies. I had seen such photographs frequently in other meditation halls in other monasteries. They are usually coloured pictures of men or women who have met with a violent death, either through murder, road accident, drowning or something of that nature. Often they show the corpse lying on the road or on the floor with the body ripped open from throat to navel, revealing all the internal organs which are sometimes pouring from the body. The head may be badly damaged with the brain splattered about, that sort of thing.

The purpose of photographs is apparently to help reduce lust (obviously important for monks, who are supposed to be celibate) though I'm not personally sure if they are of any great value even in that. Anyway, I was looking at them with no great curiosity when a young visiting monk, who could speak some English, approached me and said, 'They're horrible, aren't they?" I made no reply. He came closer and said, "They are to make you understand how disgusting the body really is and that we should not think it is beautiful".

I stared at the monk, feeling a physical tremor pass through me as a realisation, an absolute *knowing*, swept over me. What the monk had said was relatively obvious, relatively true and I knew with total conviction, ultimately quite daft.

I must have been staring at him quite intently for he stepped away from me looking uneasy. "You should meditate on beauty and ugliness," he advised and moved hurriedly to the other end of the hall.

Beauty and ugliness. Beauty *and* ugliness. But did either have any reality? Weren't they, ultimately, the same thing? Merely concepts? I looked at the photographs again. They were not ugly, nor were they beautiful. They were just the way they were. We were putting names to these states and trying to differentiate between them. But to meditate on the 'ugliness' of the body was surely to reinforce that idea. I had always understood that the whole point of meditation was to see all things in their Ultimate Truth, devoid of personal concepts. There could be nothing ultimately 'ugly' about a kidney or a spleen. In the same way, there could be nothing ultimately beautiful about a bunch of flowers: everything is just the way it is and any liking or aversion we feel is a personal and relative truth.

I decided to re-read the various translations I have of the Maha Satipatthana Sutta, the Buddha's most important teaching about meditation and whilst doing so, I realised something which struck me as both very odd and very confusing.

The Sutta is long and in its printed form, the main sections are traditionally broken up by translators into smaller sub-sections, making it easier to read and the presentation more attractive.

The Sutta gives guidance for meditation on all aspects of the body and mind. One of the sub-sections, which was of immediate interest to me, recommends that the meditator should view the body as being composed of "hairs of the head, hairs of the body, nails, teeth, skin, flesh, sinews, bones, marrow, kidneys, heart, liver, pleura, spleen, lungs, intestines, mesentery, undigested food, excrement, brain, bile, phlegm, pus, blood, sweat, fat, tears, grease, saliva, mucus, synovial fluid, urine". By contemplating the physical body in this way, we can learn to become mentally detached from it.

What surprised and confused me, and what I had never consciously noticed before in my reading, was that in each of my four translations, the sub-section was headed 'Repulsiveness of the body' or 'Loathsomeness of the body' or something similar. Repulsive? Loathsome? But surely these were relative concepts based on individual or social conditioning, our personal likes and dislikes. Although most people would probably find a dissected body spread out on a table fairly repulsive, how we would personally view it had nothing to do with what it ultimately *was*.

This all seemed very contradictory to me and I decided to seek scholarly advice.

One of the most authoritative sources in the world for information and translation of the Pali scriptures is the Pali Text Society, PTS* in Oxford. I wrote to the society asking whether the original Pali discourse contained the word 'repulsive' or 'loathsome' or any other word with a similar meaning. Their reply was unequivocal. According to the society, in the original text, the Buddha taught only that the body should be seen to be a collection of various secretions and organs — just as it is and without adding relative concepts to it. So how did this strange idea of meditating on the 'repulsiveness' of the body creep in? The PTS explained that modern translators have been influenced by the 'Visuddhimagga' (The Path of Purification) written by the 5th Century commentator, Buddhaghosa, and it was he who introduced the idea of 'repulsiveness' by using the word 'disgustingness' in his translation. The PTS concluded, "This shows the pitfalls of translators being too keen on using a 5th century commentator to interpret the text".

Buddhaghosa's commentaries have influenced the whole of modern Theravada Buddhism, not just the meditation practice. And I decided from that moment on to be extremely cautious about taking anything I read at face value but instead to keep in mind the Buddha's own words: "Do not be led by the authority of religious texts..... but *know for yourself...*"

I decided that to really understand, to know, the Buddha's teaching about the physical body I needed a corpse, lots of them in fact, as well as living bodies. I gave all this great thought and decided to write myself a 'body meditation programme' to try to investigate this aspect of the teaching as thoroughly as I could. I discussed the programme with my abbot who was very supportive and said he would arrange with the local hospital for me to have access to unidentified, unclaimed corpses, as well as to attend autopsies.

This was to be a long and complex programme, involving a total of about 15 bodies, individually, in comparative groups of different ages, in mixed groups of living and dead as well as dissected and decomposed. I thought it might take several years to complete, partly at least because of the difficulty of finding decomposed bodies, but I was in no hurry and, anyway, the programme was merely a part of my 'normal' meditation practice. But even very soon after the programme commenced, I discovered I was 'seeing' with totally different, clearer eyes and I realised it was something I should have done years ago at the very outset of my practice (though there are many practical difficulties in this type of meditation which would make it almost impossible to practise in the West). The programme also gave the rest of my meditation important new impetus.

However, despite this new impetus, there was still a niggling sense of dissatisfaction at the back of my mind. Not about the body meditation programme, but about my meditation as a whole. Not enough to cause any specific problems or doubts to arise but I was beginning to question where it was all leading. I knew where it should have been leading—but was it? It was all very well to read, in my meditation books, explanations of the expected nimittas or visions, but hallucinations, seeing lights, colours and feeling 'ripples of energy' seemed about as useful as fairy lights on a coffin. I am certainly not impatient in my meditation, but I was beginning to feel in some ways that my meditation was in danger of becoming an end in itself, rather than the means to an end. I think this may be true for many meditators.

I decided I needed guidance. I was to find it, but in a most unexpected place and time.

Even before the start of my body meditation programme, I believe I was fairly dispassionate about bodies and did not think of them as beautiful, handsome, ugly, sexy, desirable etc. except at the shallowest relative level. But as the programme progressed, I realised it had prompted my thinking to spread wider, and I found my 'clearer vision' began to encompass not just bodies but all phenomena, everything, every condition, every situation, every man-made and every *mind-made* concept.

A basic teaching of Buddhism is that 'nothing whatsoever should be clung to'. I had heard or read this phrase hundreds of times from meditation teachers and books. But it is natural for almost any practitioner to want to work first towards 'letting go' of those things, emotions and concepts which are generally thought of as 'bad' or 'undesirable' and in consequence to leave, to cultivate, and hence cling to, their opposites; the 'good' and 'desirable'. But while *any* concept of good or desirable existed, then automatically their opposites must exist also. This is good and *therefore that is bad*. But nothing whatsoever should be clung to: good or bad, desirable or undesirable. It all had to be let go off. Only when there was no clinging of any kind, only when the mind was completely freed and stilled of conceptualisation and had reached a point where all such distinctions were seen to be without foundation could there be real progress.

I had always understood this intellectually, but I found actually knowing it at the most fundamental level to be quite a different thing.

Beautiful, ugly, good, bad, happy, unhappy, clever, stupid, sane, insane, real, unreal, interesting, boring, past, future: they were all ultimately exactly the same; just concepts, and by trying to differentiate between them, we were falling into a trap. What trap?

Dualism. That was the trap. And I was in it.

I had read something, sometime ... what was it ... where was it? I searched through my bookshelves. There it was; a 40-year-old little volume; the book I had just finished reading when I met Dav in London more than a year before. I had actually read it several times but had never understood it at the right level: the intuitive level.

'The Zen teaching of Huang Po'

It is impossible to make my feelings clear as I re-read the little book and it is extremely difficult to even use Huang Po's own words to try to explain. Both in and out of context, they seem to contain paradox within paradox.

For weeks, I grappled with the riddles that the teaching of this Chinese Zen master seemed to present. Every time I thought I had reached some understanding, I also realised that my 'understanding' was shallow and based on more conceptual thinking. But what he said, his words recorded by a disciple** as he spoke them, finally began to make intellectual sense at least, though to understand Zen intellectually is really not to understand it at all. But it was a start and through Huang Po's words, I realised that although my meditation practice certainly hadn't been taking me in the wrong direction, it had been woefully incomplete. Suddenly, pieces of my meditation puzzle started to fall into place.

In our daily lives we all frequently need to make use of conceptual thinking to pass on relative truths, even Huang Po was forced to do that in trying to explain things clearly to his students. But I wasn't interested in relative truths. Relative truth does not lead to Insight Wisdom.

Although all serious meditators should try to practise continuous mindfulness of action and thought, I spent weeks watching everything I said or thought specifically looking out for dualistic and conceptual thinking. I was astonished at how deeply I was caught in the trap and how little relevance many of my thoughts had—to anything.

My meditation practice was perfectly sound but by meditating on and deliberately trying to cultivate 'good' qualities such as compassion, universal love, sympathetic joy, equanimity and all the rest, I was side-tracking myself. I might become a 'nobler', calmer person and the aim was in keeping with the Buddha's teaching, but it wouldn't take me, or anybody, a single step nearer the ultimate goal of all Buddhist meditators.

And even understanding how my emotions arose and being able to recognise and control them, ultimately had little value, it was a side-issue, for without concepts of good, bad, desirable, undesirable and so on those emotions could not arise in the first place.

Even if I meditated for a thousand years, whilst I retained the dualistic notion that 'this is good' I must also have the idea 'and that is bad'. Both would continue to exist, both were equally conceptual and both were, ultimately, a hindrance.

Of course it was 'good' to do good, to 'make merit', that was an essential aspect of Buddhism, but such activity had to be spontaneous. There could be no thought of 'if I do such and such it will be good and I will make merit, therefore I will do it'. Although the good deed would still be done, it would have entirely the wrong mental basis. It was making a concept of 'doing good'—something else to be overcome.

In one of his more straight-forward statements Huang Po said: "Away with your likes and dislikes, every single thing is just the one mind. When you have perceived this, you will have mounted the Chariot of the Buddhas".

I read the book again, and then again, trying to read it with a completely open mind, an empty mind; trying in a sense not to understand it intellectually but rather just to let Huang Po's words flow into me. "Begin to reason about it and you at once fall into error", he said.

I knew that many practitioners follow Zen partly at least because it seems to offer 'faster' results than Theravada Buddhism, which is considered by many Zen masters to be merely a primitive and undeveloped form of Buddhism. Zen, with its riddles and paradoxes, its mystic dynamism and positive expression through painting, gardens, flower arrangement and martial arts, seems to appeal to the enquiring Western mind more than Theravada which appears to be dry and passive.

But I wasn't looking for fast results. Right from the start, I had always been careful not to allow my mind to actively seek any results at all, believing that would actually be a hindrance to progress. I had already discovered for myself the value and truth of Vipassana, but after reading Huang Po's words, I realised that although I had been travelling on the main road, I had become stuck in the left-hand lane. The wisdom of Zen seemed to offer a way of moving to the middle lane, though not necessarily to the 'fast' outside lane.

Was I slowly becoming some sort of closet Zen monk? Would I eventually follow Dav and leave the orange robes of the Theravadans for the purple and yellow of Tibetan Buddhism, or the grey of Korean Zen, or whatever? I didn't think so. I was a monk and I would still be the same monk in my heart whether I was wearing orange robes, purple robes or blue Levis. I follow the Vinaya about such things but I actually couldn't care less what religious tradition or culture dictates I should wear. Theravada, Mahayana, Zen and all the rest were just labels; more concepts. I suppose I was becoming something a little different from a 'normal' Theravadan, certainly different from a normal Thai Theravadan, but I wasn't about to undergo metamorphosis into a Mahayanist. I was still a Buddhist monk, following the teaching of the Buddha. I believe that teaching included what finally came to be called Zen. Being a monk was about committing oneself to 'mind work' or 'mental cultivation', which are much better translations of the original word 'bhavana' than 'meditation'.

The place of practice, whether it be a city temple, a forest, a mountain top or a crematorium oven; the robes, whether orange, brown or purple; the rites and rituals, both of Theravada and Mahayana, were all just outward forms of limited value. They had little or nothing to do with the real work: the personal realisation of what the Buddha taught: the personal realisation of Ultimate Truth.

Huang Po said: "There is only the one mind and not a particle of anything else on which to lay hold, for this 'Mind' is the Buddha. If you students of the Way do not awake to this Mind substance, you will overlay Mind with conceptual thought, you will seek the Buddha outside yourselves, and you will remain attached to forms, pious practices and so on, all of which are harmful and not at all the way to Supreme Knowledge."

"Awaken to it, and it is there".

And so I met my teacher, or at least a guide who may perhaps eventually lead me to my teacher. Huang Po died on a mountain top in China more than a thousand years ago, but that doesn't matter. The Buddha has been dead for considerably longer. The Buddha originally pointed the way, Huang Po was another signpost on the same path.

It is only about four years since I ordained as a Buddhist monk and took my first step on the path. I have made many, many mistakes and there have been a few times when I have been discouraged, perhaps there are other such times still to come. But I am still *trying*. Perhaps I have so far learned only a little and I know I have a great deal more still to learn. However, I believe every day, every small step, gives me a little more genuine understanding of what the Buddha taught. And I am happy, I am sabbai, to continue the journey.

*The Pali Text Society was founded in 1881. It has published the entire Pali Canon in Roman script as well as most of it in English. All the major commentaries have been published in Romanised Pali and a number of these have also been translated into English. The Society also publishes a Pali-English and an English-Pali dictionary.

** Huang Po's words were recorded by his student P'ei Hsiu. They were translated and edited by John Blofeld in 1947.

My good friend and teacher Phra Maha Laow at
Wat Buddhapadipa in London.

The view from my kuti at Wat Nahoob—the multiple peaks of Khao Nor.

The Uposatha Hall of Wat Buddhapadipa in London.

The monks' residence at Wat Buddhapadipa.

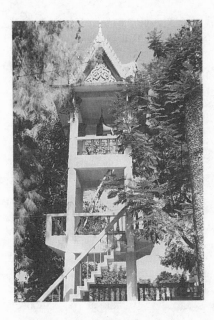

Wat Nahoob's bell tower.

Phra Maha Weera and a little Nahoobian.

Yom My on the step of my kuti at Wat Nahoob.

A cross between a little Swiss chalet and a garden shed—my kuti at Wat Nahoob.

My meditation platform at Wat Nahoob with a Tibetan
'wishing prayer' about impermanence nailed above.

A 'ramwong' in progress during an ordination ceremony at Wat Nahoob.

Then still unused—Wat Nahoob's new crematorium.

Funeral display at Wat Nahoob.

Acharn Waow, the abbot of Wat Nahoob, receiving his ritual
wash from villagers on Songkran Day.

Village ladies at Wat Nahoob on Songkran Day.

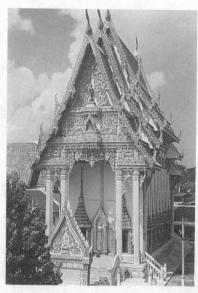

The Bote, or Uposatha Hall, of Wat Worranatbanpot.

The ancient chedi at Wat Worranatbanpot.

The author with the abbot of
Wat Worranatbanpot, Phra Suthee Thammasopon.

My kuti at Wat Worranatbanpot.

Glossary

Abhidhamma (n.)   Buddhist Metaphysics.

Acharn (n.)   From Acariya. It means teacher.

AE   Anjan Era.

Anjali (n.)   A position of the hands where the palms are placed together in a prayer-like manner.

Arahant (n.)   A person whose mind has passed beyond such defiling emotions as hatred, ill-will, pride, etc. and who has achieved the highest levels of wisdom.

Antaravasaka (n.)   (referred to as 'sabong' in Thailand) A Theravadan monk's inner, sarong-like robe.

Bote (n.)   (or Uposatha Hall) A large hall in a Buddhist temple which houses the principal Buddha image of the temple.

Chedi (n.)   A pagoda which contains relics of the Buddha or of highly-respected followers of the Buddha.

Civara (Pali) (n.)   (referred to as 'Jivorn' in Thailand) A Theravadan monk's outer robe.

C of E (n.)   The Church of England (protestant, Anglican)

Dhamma (Pali)(n. or adj.) One aspect of the Triple Gem. It means the
Dharma (skt.)   Truth within the teachings or (more superficially) the texts which record teachings about that truth.

Farang (n. or adj.)   Light-skinned, non-Thai. The first Westerners to visit Thailand were from France. The French pronunciation of 'Farançais' developed into the form 'Farang'.

Jivorn (skt.) (n.)   A Theravadan monk's outer robe.
(Civara) (Pali)

Khao Pansa (v. phrase) To enter into the rainy season retreat. Here it is often shortened to Pansa. This period starts in July and lasts untils October. Traditionally, a monk must stay in one temple for the duration of the rainy season retreat. The time is spent studying, meditating and remaining in close contact with the teacher. The length of time that a monk has remained in the robes is calculated according to the number of rainy season retreats he has completed.

(adj. and n.) The day marking the beginning of the rainy season retreat. This day follows Magga Puja day.

Kuti (n.) A monk's or nun's living quarters. It is often a small, basic, one-roomed wooden house.

Looksit (n.) Follower or sometimes student.

Maha (adj.) Great.

Mahadhatu (n.) Great element. In the case of Wat Mahadhatu, the great element referred to is copper. One of the main Buddha images in this temple is housed within a copper enclosure, thus giving rise to the name of the temple.

Nibbana (Pali) Enlightenment.
Nirvana (skt.) (n.)

Ork Pansa (v. or n.) The end of the rainy season retreat.

Pali (n.or adj.) An ancient Indian dialect. The earliest known Buddhist scriptures were recorded in Pali.

Pansa (n.) Rainy season.

Phra (n.) Generally a Buddhist monk. However, it can also mean a high-ranking respected person, often with royal connections.

Phra Maha A title given to a monk who has successfully completed at least three of the nine levels of Pali studies.

Pracane (v.) To offer food to a monk. All food and other requisites must be offered formally by a layperson to a monk.

Sabbai (adj.) Content, comfortable, happy.

Sala (n.) Thai-style pavillion with open sides, which offers protection from the sun and a place to rest. Salas are often found in temples.

Sanghati (n.) A Theravadan monk's robe which is folded and hung over the left shoulder during formal ceremonies.

Sanuk (adj.) Fun, amusing, pleasantly diverting.

Songkran (n. or adj.) The Traditional Thai New Year. The official date is April 13, however the holiday period is often extended to three or five days.

Thera (n.) Elder, a monk who has spent at least ten years in the robes.

Theravada (n.) The doctrine of the Elders. The form of Buddhism practised in many south-east Asian countries such as Thailand, Sri Lanka, Burma and Cambodia.

The Triple Gem (n.) The Buddha, the Great Teacher; the Dhamma, the Truth and; the Sangha, the community of followers.

Ungsa (n.) A Theravadan monk's simple one-shouldered waistcoat.

Upachaya (n.) Preceptor, the officiating monk at an ordination ceremony.

Upasaka (n.) Devout layman.

Upasika (n.) Devout laywoman.

Vinaya (n.) The discipline (rules) of the ordained Sangha. The books which list the rules.

The author's royalties from sales of this book are dedicated to

Phra Peter Pannapadipo's Students' Education Trust

A fund was established in 1994 by friends of Phra Peter in the UK to help a particularly clever Thai student who had gained a university place but could not afford the fees. More than enough was donated so the balance became the foundation of a Trust dedicated to helping other impoverished Thai students.

The Trust Fund remains very small, but since 1994 (to July 1997) 30 Thai students have been supported, most of them studying at universities or technical and vocational colleges. Nearly all the SET-supported students are from very poor rice-farming families. Without the Trust's help most would have been unable to take up their de-served college or university places. Some of those already in higher education would have been forced to drop out and return to work in the family rice paddies, or find some other mundane dead-end job. With the Trust's support the students are <u>achieving</u>—achieving some-thing for themselves and for the future of their country.

The Trust helps students in different ways. For example:
* New students who have passed entrance examinations for universities or colleges but who cannot take up their places because of family poverty.
* Students already in higher education who may be forced to drop out, unable to pay further fees.
* Students already in higher education who face some temporary difficulty or unexpected expense and who need support only for a term or two.
* Students who need support of some other kind—for books, uniform, tools, travel or specialised educational aids.

Students at university currently receive annual fee grants of 6,000 Baht, while those at technical and vocational colleges receive 3,000 Baht annually. Non-fee grants may be made depending entir-ely on individual needs.

Higher education in Thailand is relatively inexpensive, but there are still many bright, diligent and deserving students who cannot afford even the modest fees. The Thai government has recently introduced a student loan scheme but many are ineligible to apply. The Students' Education Trust can help only a very few of these disadvantaged students but wants to do all it can for as many as possible. Even a small donation goes a long way in education in Thailand and can make a big difference to the future of a bright boy or girl.

If you are interested in knowing more about the Students' Education Trust, and how you can help a deserving Thai student, please write to:

Phra Peter Pannapadipo, Wat Worranatbanpot, Thammavitee Road, Amphur Muang, Nakhon Sawan 60000, Thailand.